CERAMIC TO CLAY

The mother of a severely brain-injured son searches for authentic healing

By Sharon Dzialo

First published by Dog Ear Publishing
4010 W. 86th Street, Ste H
Indianapolis, IN 46268
www.dogearpublishing.net

ISBN: 978-160844-758-9

This book is printed on acid-free paper.

Printed in the United States of America

DEDICATED TO

PHIL, ADAM, and AIMEE DZIALO

INTRODUCTION

An unexpected event occurred—in this case, my son's near-drowning—and I was provided with an opportunity to open my life in previously unimaginable ways. As my family joined my son on his long road to recovery, time and again, we had experiences that triggered growth and healing. My husband and I were called upon each day to expand our world of personal beliefs to reach into the unknown. We searched for people with vision and sustained abilities. Life was constantly provoking.

Adam's recovery has been long and slow. Many people who initially stood by us became impatient and moved on with their lives. Some lost faith, accepted what was, and never believed in what could be. Our small family learned to open our minds and hearts to recognize the unlimited possibilities and power that we possess over any situation. The purpose of Adam's accident has not been to confine or limit us but rather to set us free.

In this book I have attempted to document some of the most significant experiences and memories from the past 11 years. For me, the greatest lesson garnered from this big life has been about the true nature of healing. The entire family needed to heal, and that healing, I discovered, would happen only if we were willing to go deeply into the process, wherever that would take us. We took many side trips, both interesting and difficult. I was always motivated by the belief that if I was willing to do my work, I could be present for Adam more fully, because originally, I believed that he needed me more than I needed him. I am not of this opinion now. Adam has been my teacher and my inspiration.

Son nearly drowned, spent 20 to 25 minutes underwater.
Severely brain-injured at age 12 ½.
Daughter, age 14 ½, entering high school.

Intensive Care—three weeks. In-patient Rehab—six weeks.
Home. Dining room converted into hospital room.
Aides, therapists, round-the-clock care.

Traditional therapies: speech, physical, occupational. . . .
Rehab specialists, botox, splints, casting, surgery, medication.
FRUSTRATION AND FEAR.

Nontraditional therapies: clairvoyance, homeopathy, angels,
acupuncture, body-mind centering, massage, sound-healing,
craniosacral, chiropractic, Johrei, shiatsu, hyperbaric oxygen,
neuro-biofeedback, cell salts, ABR, psychotherapy, past-life
readings, soul astrology. SOFTER, KINDER, DEEPER.

Son returned to school with full-time aide. Mother back
to work after two years at home. Untenable juggling act.
Bankruptcy and lawsuit. Daughter left for college.

Early retirement for mother;
more possibilities for son and time for daughter.
Lawsuit settled. House on the market. Husband retired.
Apology offered and accepted.

Moved to the ocean. New beginning.
Eleven years have passed.
Bare bones of the story. The inner story is the only story.

THE FIRST DAY

I awoke to a beautiful summer morning. I had an eight-week break from my job as a high school counselor. A long to-do list awaited me, most of the activities related to my younger child, my son, Adam. On Sunday, he was to leave for a hockey camp at Providence College in Rhode Island. A large duffle bag was lying open in his bedroom, overflowing with clothes, supplies, hockey equipment, and a few surprises. This would be his first week-long experience away from home. He was excited and nervous, and I was an anxious mother. Sleepovers were difficult for him. I half anticipated checking into a hotel near Providence College so he would feel safer. I shouldn't have been so worried, because he was attending this camp with his good friend, Stephen. Both had been playing hockey for at least five years. Adam had chosen the position of goalie and demonstrated great skills. Just that year, we had customized a helmet for him with the words "no fear" and a tiger's roaring mouth.

I planned to pick him up later that day. He had been attending an adventure camp at the local community college and was just returning from an overnight camping trip. After the pick-up, we were going to head directly to a baseball tournament. He was playing for an all-star team, and though hockey was his favorite sport, baseball was a close second.

I was filled with thoughts of my boy this day, missing him and wondering how tired and cranky he would be after this adventure and more adventures to come. Adam liked to keep busy, so this kind of schedule was nothing unusual for him.

The day was proceeding according to schedule. My 14-year-old daughter, Aimee, was working at the YMCA. She called to say that she needed a ride home. I left as my husband, Philip, arrived home from work. He then received the phone call that all parents dread with every fiber of their being. Adam was at Baystate Trauma Center. He had been in a swimming accident, and his condition was critical. Phil was told not to come alone. He got in the car and searched for me as I was driving Aimee home. We delivered Aimee to a friend's house and headed to the hospital.

I drove. I don't remember what we did with the other car. I remember thinking that I was in better shape than Phil. He just kept repeating the words, "Don't come alone. Don't come alone." I focused on driving and was distracted by only a sickening feeling in the pit of my stomach. I wasn't sure that I could make it to the hospital without vomiting.

Minutes before we arrived at the hospital and I could actually see it directly in front of us, I experienced a strange feeling. I felt "flooded with calm." I looked at Phil and said, "Adam is still with us. I would know if he was not. . ." I could not have been more certain of anything.

We parked the car directly in front of the emergency room, where a social worker was waiting for us. She explained the seriousness of Adam's condition and the circumstances of the accident. No one from the camp was there. The doctors at the trauma center were attempting to stabilize him. It was critical; he had been underwater for a very long time.

The social worker then left us alone in a closed room—no one to talk with, no one to question. Phil and I just kept looking at each other, repeating what we knew. We could not make any sense out of this incredibly frightening turn of events. I remember feeling intense cold. I could not warm myself. I kept asking for blankets, wrapping myself as I paced back and forth.

Finally, the social worker returned. It felt like many hours had passed. She informed us that Adam had been stabilized enough to move him to the Pediatric Intensive Care Unit. He was on a ventilator and had been placed in a medically induced coma. We didn't and couldn't understand any of this. Adam was going to his baseball tournament; he would be late. We were invited to accompany Adam in the elevator with his doctors.

My son, my Adam, lay on a stretcher. His eyes were closed, and he looked puffy and gray. He was receiving oxygen, and two doctors were monitoring his transport. One doctor was very kind. He spoke compassionately and encouraged us to touch and kiss Adam. I was screaming silently, *No, no, this is not my son. My son is not on this stretcher, not in a coma. I need to leave now to pick him up at the community college. He's going to be late for his game.* This child on the stretcher was Adam, but he wasn't Adam. He bore little resemblance to the wiry, hyper, athletic 12-year-old we had said good-bye to yesterday morning. He felt untouchable—too cold, too gray, too far away. He was freezing; I was freezing.

Phil leaned against the wall of the elevator and crumpled over, weeping. Those tears poured out for days. He would look at me and say, "I can't stop crying. . ." He felt totally out of control; he was inconsolable. I had never before witnessed this depth of emotion in my husband.

We settled in with Adam in a private room in the ICU. Our watch began; we were afraid to look away from the monitors that registered continued signs of life in this pale, silent son. Machines were holding him steady. I heard the words, "The next seventy-two hours are the most critical." The doctors were most concerned about fluid building up in his brain, the "secondary assault" so common in brain injuries. Several CAT scans were done. Adam missed that second assault. What did all this mean?

Phil, Aimee, and I settled into a huge chair at the foot of Adam's bed. Aimee was to begin high school in a few months. None of this made sense to her. She did not want her brother to die, and she questioned us constantly. We could not assure her with answers. We held each other, watched the monitors, watched Adam breathe, and waited. I remember sitting there, closing my eyes, and reaching deep inside to search again and again for that "flooding of calm." Each and every time, I found it. Though I shed many tears and I felt intense anxiety, I never spiraled down into the deepest place of grief and unimaginable fear. As long as I could find this "calm," I believed that Adam was with us and would stay with us. I did not, however, have any idea what to expect from his brain injury. When he opened his eyes, what would we see? What would he see?

THE ACCIDENT

We asked many questions. We hired an investigator. The college hired several investigators. The media dug out the details. Each person held a piece of the story. Neither my husband nor I were present at the scene, but I am Adam's mother and knew and know things about my son. No one ever asked me.

This is what I believed happened on July 24, 1998, on the Deerfield River. Fourteen 12-year-old boys and two counselors were cleaning up the campsite after spending a night out at a local state forest. This day wrapped up a week of outdoor adventures. The counselors (a young man and a young woman) and the boys gathered their equipment, corralled the boys together, and set off in the van to return home. They had time for one more adventure before they were due back at the college for pick-up by the parents. According to the counselors, this particular group of boys were not interested in a hike; instead, they chose to stop by the Deerfield River and practice a rescue maneuver. One counselor took half of the boys upstream to act as the victims. They were to wait for a signal and then jump into the river and float feet-first downstream. The other boys were waiting at a designated spot, watching for the victims and throwing out bags at the appropriate time to the floating boys, who would then be pulled to safety.

The boys took turns as victims and rescuers. They were aware that at any point they had the option not to participate. The counselors were comfortable with the flow of the river, having previously checked for the anticipated release of water from a dam upstream. This particular area of the river is widely used by rafters and canoeists for the thrill of paddling in the increasing current after the release of the water.

Then some unthinkable events unraveled. One of the boys needed to leave early and one counselor decided to accompany him. The male counselor drove this boy and one of his friends away from the site, leaving 12 boys with the young female counselor. According to the female counselor's written statement, she and her coworker had discussed leaving only one counselor on-site to continue the exercise with the other boys and both had been comfortable with this decision. She remained and placed herself with the rescuers within eyesight of the group of victims. Not all of the remaining boys chose to participate. Some of the boys had tired of the exercise, and others felt the water was too cold. Adam, having already successfully executed a float, decided he would try one more time. He stepped in front of one of his reluctant friends and jumped into the water when he was given the proper signal.

At this point in my rendition of the events of this day, I tune in to my mother's intuition about what might have happened in my son's mind after he hit the water. Adam found himself in a rapidly increasing current as the upstream dam released a huge bubble of water. A river guide reported that Adam was almost sitting up, his head raised. He then raised his hand. Someone who was actually watching the river exercise wondered if Adam was fooling around, showing off. My gut tells me something entirely different. I believe that he was afraid; he felt the increased current and lost all sense of what he should do under those conditions. He was afraid to put his head down; he was afraid, and he put his hand up to motion for help. His position in the water was very awkward, and he could not straighten out. Initially, I believe, the boys were told to be in a reclining floating position with their feet headed in the direction of the rescue group. Adam then made the decision that would change the course of his life. He tried to stand up, to stop himself. His foot somehow became trapped, and he was pulled under. No amount of maneuvering could disengage him from this spot. He came up from below the water a few times and then stayed down, his head and body pulled forward.

I know my son. Even at the age of 12, he could not hide his fears. Though he could stand in front of a goalie net and take shot after shot, stopping them with his stick, or glove or goalie pads on his knees, he was afraid of things. He could not stay in the house by himself; he couldn't even stay on a floor of the house by himself. He needed to know someone was close by. He had trouble sleeping by himself. He would never swim in our pool without someone near him. His fears were clear and deep. Oh sure, he had "fearless" inscribed on his goalie helmet and he wore "fearless" t-shirts, but his father and I knew a different boy.

I mention all of this because I am absolutely certain that my son did not choose to be reckless on that day at the river. His actions were based entirely on fear, and no investigator nor river guide can make me believe any other possible scenario.

When it was obvious that Adam was in serious trouble, the counselor attempted to swim out to him, only to be thwarted by the current. This part of the story was corroborated by our investigator. Rafts began showing up in the area. Twenty-one boats in two separate groups all came through this site, and at least one raft floated right over Adam's submerged body. The rafters and their guides pulled over to the side, disembarked, and ran to help with the rescue. They formed a human chain to reach him, but the current was too strong. There were many experienced river people at the site, and their efforts were fruitless. The minutes were passing, and Adam was no closer to a rescue. He was submerged at this point for at least five minutes.

Finally, someone suggested creating a tag line. Guides and dozens of rafters were used as anchors, holding a rope that stretched from shore to shore. The rescuers used a hand-over-hand maneuver to move toward Adam. One guide reached Adam, gripped Adam's life jacket, and pulled as hard as he could, but Adam's foot remained trapped, keeping him underwater. Adam had been underwater for 15 minutes.

The rescuers tried one last maneuver. Trees were used to anchor the ropes, pulling the line taut. Four men attached a raft to the line and moved as close to Adam as they could. One of the men reached down from the firmly positioned raft and completely embraced the top part of Adam's body. He reached Adam's head first and began rescue breathing immediately while two other men pulled Adam free of the entrapment.

Twenty-five minutes underwater. People at the scene had called 911, and emergency personnel had already arrived. Adam was immediately transferred to an ambulance and taken to a waiting helicopter. He was not breathing, but the defibrillator signaled that his heart could be restarted. The helicopter flew him to the local trauma center, emergency personnel providing CPR the entire time. Adam had no pulse upon his arrival at the hospital, but the doctors revived him and were attempting to stabilize him when we arrived at the hospital approximately two and a half hours after the accident.

A rescuer with many years of life-saving experience who had been at the scene reported that generally when people are pulled from the water after drowning or near-drowning, their faces are caught in masques of terror. In absolute contrast, Adam's facial expression was serene.

JILLIAN'S ANGEL

One of my most poignant memories from Adam's three weeks in the Intensive Care Unit at Baystate Medical Center actually involved another family. When we first arrived on the unit with Adam, we noticed nothing through our haze of shock but what was happening in his room. He was in a private room, and we held a steady vigil by his bedside. The doctors and nurses came in and out frequently, monitored the numbers, and straightened the lines pumping fluids through his ravaged body.

As we settled into a type of routine, if that even sounds remotely possible under the circumstances, we became aware of the other patients and their families. One family in particular attracted our attention. A young woman named Jillian was in a private room down the hall. We would notice her parents and other family members as they walked by Adam's room. It soon became obvious that they recognized my husband. Jillian was a student at the high school where my husband was the principal. That connection and our children's serious medical conditions forged a bond between us. Jillian had cancer, diagnosed and treated in late stage. She was in a very precarious state. Doctors were trying everything in an attempt to save this young woman's life.

Adam's situation had stabilized, so we had begun to breathe a little, though we knew nothing about the extent of his brain injury. He was in a medically induced coma, and we were waiting. Each time I saw Jillian's parents I recognized my husband and me—parents desperately seeking our children's survival. We would chat briefly in the hallway, never wanting to be too far away from our children. We smiled at each other every morning, briefly asking, "How did the night go?" We were walking through the minutes, hours, and days together.

One day—and I don't know how long our families were together in this space and time, because the days were just a blur of fear, fatigue, questions, and few answers—we realized that Jillian's condition had worsened. We saw more doctors and nurses entering her room. Her visitors were limited to her immediate family. They would hurry past Adam's room in shock and tears. We paced inside Adam's room, watching and listening. We were afraid to look, to listen, to speak, to know. Would this be our journey too?

Couldn't anyone help this young woman? Could anyone save her? Every possible intervention had been attempted. The cancer was insidious, the treatments incredibly potent and harsh. Jillian's organs were shutting down.

I met Jillian once, when her mother brought me into her room. There were angels everywhere—pictures, paintings, porcelain figurines. Jillian was passionate about angels. She painted them and collected them, and people gifted them to her. I walked slowly around her room, trying to get some sense of who she was. She had lain in her bed, and I quietly greeted her though she was unable to respond. I remember wondering why she embraced these angels with such intensity.

Philip and I had only recently been introduced to angels as symbols of protection, strength, and healing. People would come to visit us in the early days at the hospital and whisper about the angels' presence, pleading with us to pray to them to fill our life at this desperate time.

The energy on the unit on the day of Jillian's decline felt electrified. We saw the serious faces of the hospital personnel, sensing their frustration, sadness, and grief. We, too, were filled with deep and profound compassion for Jillian's family.

As we watched from the sanctity of our still-breathing–son's room, we also felt some guilt. Should we be feeling curious? Why were we being pulled so powerfully in their direction? This family deserved complete privacy. Should we have shut the door? Should we have reached out to them? How could we, enmeshed in our own torturous pain and shock, reach out to this family? I remember so clearly that I wanted to. I could not deny the connection that I felt with them. Safely ensconced in the quiet solitude of Adam's room, I tried to imagine this family's last minutes with their precious daughter, this mother and father kissing their daughter for the last time in the final acceptance that her life was over. I sat with this harsh reality. I was heartbroken for Jillian's parents yet consumed with fear for Adam; Adam's hold on life was still so tentative. I could not move.

There was a knock on the door. The hospital social worker requested that Philip step into the hall for a moment. Jillian's father stood there, unable to enter Adam's room. Out of sight, father to father, Jillian's father removed an angel that he had faithfully worn on his shirt throughout his daughter's illness. He handed the angel to Phil—to wear it, to believe in it, and, most importantly, to honor his daughter's life. My husband walked back into the room with the angel pinned on his shirt and tears streaming down his face.

I was absolutely awestruck by this man's action. He had just witnessed his daughter's death, yet for one brief moment, he stepped away from his intense grief and offered this gift to our family. He was passing on strength, one father to another, knowing what Phil would need to move through this life-and-death journey of his own.

Some time later, we received a copy of one of Jillian's angel drawings. I loved it immediately, framed it, and placed it near Adam's bed. The angel is beautiful—stately, wearing a long blue gown and standing among billowy clouds. I see her every day. And every day, I am reminded of this family's loss and their incredibly generous spirit.

THE HOSPITAL EXPERIENCES

Adam remained in the Intensive Care Unit for three weeks. They carefully removed him from the ventilator, weaning him slowly when they witnessed his continued laborious breathing. He was coaxed out of the medically induced coma and stabilized. The head doctor of the unit, a kind man, told us that Adam was ready to be moved to a rehabilitation facility. During Adam's stay at the trauma center, we always felt that he was in the right place. The staff handled our family gently, protected us from the onslaught of media and well-wishers, and provided us with a place to stay overnight. They made us feel safe.

The next experience at a rehabilitation hospital in Connecticut was the beginning of a very difficult time. This facility was within a reasonable driving distance to Greenfield, our hometown . We never left Adam alone. I would spend the weekdays with Adam, and Phil would stay with him over the weekend. Aimee was 14 years old and about to begin her first year of high school. She yearned for some summer-type activities. She vacationed with friends, worked a bit, and spent time with me at home on the weekends.

Images flood my memory from those six interminably long weeks. An MRI was taken in the middle of the night, and the results were offered the next day by a dark-haired, squat, middle-aged neurologist dressed all in black. She said, "Well, he's awake and there is some brain activity." I had no idea what those words meant. Was this good news or bad? She uttered the words without any feeling, just as pure fact. She was sensitive enough not to discuss the results in my son's room so she guided me into an empty hospital room where I sat in a chair surrounded by this doctor and her underlings. Not once did she acknowledge that this must be a difficult time, nor did she recognize that I was completely alone, without the support of my husband, family, or friends. She left, and I sat with her words, in shock and confusion. What did it mean? Of course, I went to the worst possible place, imagining that she had just presented me with horrific news. I did not want to call her back for further explanation; I never wanted to see her again. I assumed from her cold, objective demeanor that she didn't care, that she was just doing her job.

The next day, I told one of the nurses that I needed a new neurologist. How I had the presence of mind to request this, I will never understand. They sent me a very kind man who led me into the hallway directly outside Adam's room and drew me pictures of the brain injury. I looked at him and then I looked at his picture. I said, "Look at all of the areas of the brain that are not injured." He agreed with me and gently explained that Adam's oxygen deprivation from his near-drowning had caused a mid-brain injury, specifically to the basal ganglia. To access the higher brain functions, he said, it was necessary to connect through the mid-brain. This was a big problem, and he did not know what the outcome would be—mild or severe. He never trampled me with too much information. I was taking in only what I was ready to hear. In my traumatized state, I continued to focus on the fact that much was unknown about the brain, which to me meant "possibility." When it was time for Adam to leave the rehab hospital, this neurologist visited one last time and said, "I will pray for your son."

We also had our first exposure to the traditional approach to rehabilitation. Adam was assigned a physical therapist who pulled him out of bed, even though he was too stiff to really sit in a wheelchair with any degree of comfort, and positioned him in a stander. The therapists told me that they were trying to "break his tone." An occupational therapist wheeled Adam to a computer and used his spasm-wracked and contracted arm to play a game. It was "important to stimulate him," she said. We saw several different speech therapists. During our short six-week stay, the speech staff turnover was nonstop. Each therapist would attempt the same tracking exercises, communication cards, and oral motor work, but Adam was so deeply in brain fog that he would look right through them.

Before we left the trauma center, a tube had been inserted into Adam's stomach because he was unable to take anything orally. The smelly, thick formula pumped directly into his stomach will never leave my olfactory memory. Adam was tube fed 24 hours a day, "to keep him alive" they would explain, never focusing on his inability to rest because his body was working 24 hours a day to process the feedings. I could not understand any of this, yet I knew no other way. My immediate responsibility at the rehab facility was to learn how to operate the pump.

There was a meeting scheduled a few weeks after Adam's arrival at this second hospital with all of the members of the rehabilitation team. After the heartless meeting with the first neurologist, I remember feeling completely out of control and fearful. I had handed my son's care over to a group of people whom I thought may be able to find ways to help him. I met with the head of the team before the meeting and requested a favor: I wanted to run the meeting, and the only thing that I wanted to discuss was how this hospital and these people could help my son. I began the meeting by introducing myself to the group and shared some of my husband's and my own life experiences. We were professionals, committed parents, and educated consumers and would do whatever we needed to do to take care of our son. They listened politely, offered little, and later informed us that we would be preparing to take Adam home. The message? "We cannot help your son."

Shortly after this meeting, Adam became very sick. He had developed pneumonia from a hospital-borne bacteria. My husband and I had become increasingly uncomfortable with his respiration, as he was struggling, coughing, and very uncomfortable. The hospital did tests but could not identify the problem. Adam went into shock and was immediately moved to the Intensive Care Unit on another floor of this rehab hospital. I remember standing with the pediatric specialist who headed Adam's treatment team. I was alone, waiting for Phil to arrive after he had received the second worst phone call of his life: "Adam is in trouble, come right away." I was understandably upset and fearful; I looked at the doctor and whispered, "Oh, God, not the ventilator again."

The doctor heard my words and thought that I was requesting that no extraordinary methods be used this time to save Adam's life. I was not saying this; I merely did not want my son to be traumatized again. I realized in a shocking way how easy it was to have my intentions completely misunderstood. Adam spent two days in this ICU and then returned to his original room. He never did need the ventilator.

Amidst this chaos, I do recall a few profound experiences that I treasure with great fondness and respect. One morning, a Hispanic aide entered Adam's room. She asked if she might pray over Adam. I nodded and said, "of course". She then told me that she had a gift and perhaps she could help. I watched as she gently placed her hands on Adam, and I listened to the beautiful sounds of her Spanish prayer.

I held Adam's head in my hands every day, saying the same prayer. I prayed to bring healing light to my son, and I visualized the light as it moved through his severely injured brain. I desperately wanted to believe that my prayers could heal my son.

Most days, weather permitting, I took Adam out of bed, transferred him to a wheelchair, and pushed him outside. We would take the elevator down to the ground floor and walk away from the hospital into a beautiful meditation garden. I would push his wheelchair into the gazebo to protect him from the sun, and we would sit. He was not comfortable in this chair, and he was not comfortable in his bed. I only wanted to find a place of peace for us. When we left the gazebo, I always pushed Adam past memorial statues, mostly angels, dedicated to children who had left this life. I never felt sad as I read the markers; I felt companionship.

Some days I would read, and I found myself drawn to books about healing. All I remember is this one phrase: "Some miracles happen quickly; others happen over a long period of time." I knew that Adam's miracle would happen over a long time.

HOME

We left the hospital in Connecticut after six weeks, hardly prepared, hardly equipped on any level. I wanted Adam home; I wanted to be home, but I had no experience caring for a severely injured person. I would continue to retreat to that place of calm inside myself and would hear the whisper: "Adam will be okay." I still felt deep fear and insecurity.

In preparation for Adam's release from the hospital, the staff helped us arrange for a home visit. The purpose was to "test the waters"—to help us figure out what we needed to change in our home environment to adequately care for our son. Basically, we needed a hospital room inside our home. Just getting Adam's rigid body into our car was supremely challenging. No one had suggested that we might need a wheelchair van or even an ambulance to get him home safely. We were getting a crash course in the difficulties involved in caring for someone in a typically furnished home and driving an unmodified vehicle.

In anticipation of this home visit, we had merely set up a twin bed in the living room piled with pillows. We were unable to make Adam comfortable. When we returned to the hospital after the visit, we had plenty of grist for the mill. My husband set about ordering a hospital bed, turning our dining room into Adam's new bedroom, and contacting agencies for feeding equipment and supplies. All of this confusion and utter frustration with our ignorance about our son's needs did not dissuade us from our decision. We were bringing Adam home. We knew that he needed to be safe at home.

When Adam was eventually discharged from the rehab hospital, I honestly could not say that he was any better than when he initially entered that hospital. He had sustained a serious case of pneumonia and still suffered from some respiratory issues. I wondered about the staff at this hospital; had they held out any hope for Adam's recovery? Had they discharged him into our care so he could die at home in our care? Or had they recognized our strength and commitment to Adam and released him because we were his best chance?

Before we arrived home, a friend built a wheelchair ramp in our garage. He was a carpenter by trade and had been one of Adam's hockey coaches. His son was Adam's friend. He shared with us sometime later that this job was one of the most difficult tasks of his life. He had three sons, all active and healthy. He had also been fond of Adam and had respected his athletic prowess as a goalie on the team.

Phil was busy removing all of the furniture from the dining room—the room with a big table and many memories of holiday celebrations of sumptuous turkey dinners. He repainted the room and decorated it with posters, pictures of angels, and a very silly drawing that Adam had wanted of himself with characters from the animated series *South Park*. We had been to Maine a few weeks before the accident, and this drawing made all of us laugh, so we framed it in honor of Adam. Phil placed a hospital bed to one side of the room, a pole with the pump for Adam's feeding tube near the bed, and a cot for one of us to sleep with Adam. The room was ready.

I left the hospital barely comfortable with Adam's feeding process. He was to be fed around the clock, the fluid pumped into his stomach through a tube every four hours. Mechanical things always intimidated me, yet I had to get comfortable with this or I could not sustain my son's life; he was totally dependent on this nourishment. I had to learn how to move this rigid body—change him, turn him, reposition him, and bathe him. This was my boy, my Adam, my easy baby. I had cradled and bathed and rocked him to sleep—my curly-haired, blonde, blue-eyed boy. Now I felt insecure handling my own son.

The first months were filled with memories of nurses and nurse's aides. We were unfamiliar with having strangers in our home—no privacy and no normalcy. We were inundated with cards, letters, and prayers.

"Call if you need anything."

"Our thoughts and prayers are with you."

"Let us know if we can help."

Dinners were delivered once a week. It was wonderful and kept us connected to the community. The doorbell would ring, and we would be greeted by a different community member each time. The challenge we were facing seemed enormous, and we couldn't fathom being alone with it. We felt deep gratitude for this generosity and connection.

Adam's friends were present during that first year. They visited, sent get-well cards, and brought pumpkins and a Christmas tree. They promised to walk with Adam through his recovery.

Adam's 13th birthday was the last one celebrated by his friends. His January birthday came at a very difficult time—Adam was rigid, traumatized, and suffering. He was plagued by muscle spasms; his sleep was seriously disturbed; his body was pulling into contraction. He would look at people, but he seemed to be looking through them.

Still, his friends wanted to give him a birthday party. They appeared during a terrible snowstorm. Most of the cars could not make it up the driveway. The guests dragged themselves through the snow, carrying a cake, cards, and presents. I remember how vibrant and full of life they all looked as they entered Adam's room. They gathered around Adam's bed, opened his presents for him, and read their cards out loud.

Adam was there, but he was not there. For most of the boys, this was their last visit. Thinking of this day would often fill me with sadness because his friends left with a terrifying and sad image of Adam.

The connection with community and the visits from friends diminished over time, and after the first year, very few were able to sustain a relationship with us. I waited many times for the phone to ring, but this waiting led to nothing but pain. I wondered often why this journey with my son was fraught with such loneliness. To be truthful, it had been difficult to accept and enjoy the early attention because my husband and I had been in such a state of shock. When the shock wore off and our son began his slow healing journey, we could have and would have enjoyed more attention. By then, however, people were too sad, too afraid, too uncomfortable, too guilty, too busy, too overwhelmed, and perhaps too impatient to come back.

Evenings were lonely; weekends were lonely. The gray shadows of depression infiltrated our life. I had never before known or anticipated the soul-wrenching darkness of loneliness. I wept bitter tears.

In those silent hours of the day and night, I often found myself praying earnestly for Adam to heal, body, mind, and spirit. On some level, I recognized quickly that physical healing would never be enough and that we were being drawn to a place where something far deeper needed to be addressed as well. No path was immediately apparent, however. How would I find the way?

TERRI

The first year was full of shock and undulating waves of the relentless layers of trauma. Many people would ask us, "How can you do this?" We didn't think about it; we just did it. We came home from our rehabilitation experience deeply entrenched in Western medicine's approach to brain injury. We were offered medication and surgery, one procedure after another—botox, splinting, serial casting, surgical release of tendons. The results were never satisfying. We just kept turning our broken son over to the experts, pleading with them to fix Adam, to make him whole again. We could very easily have gotten lost during this time, turning all decisions over to the doctors and therapists. We were waiting for the magic bullet, the ultimate recovery tool. The doctors made no promises, and they offered no hope. They went through the motions of the "tried and true" and said little else.

It was not enough. Adam desperately needed something more. We slowly moved into the world of the nontraditional approach to healing—healing, not fixing. We proceeded with cautious excitement, surrounding Adam with people who would seek his potential and not use words like "limitation," "custodial care," and "irreversible brain damage."

A friend who was a nurse and someone I had worked with professionally for many years offered a few possibilities. I trusted her, and we soon had the privilege and the honor of meeting Terri, a woman who would have an immense impact on all of our lives. She was described to us as a clairvoyant. Neither my husband nor I had any previous experience or knowledge of anyone who had this kind of perception, the ability to see beyond the range of natural vision. We had nothing to lose and everything to gain. Our first meeting with Terri took place soon after Adam was discharged from the hospital.

What follows is Terri's own story about our first meeting. It is truly remarkable, and I could never do justice to this story with my own words. She graciously and respectfully recounted her experience.

MEETING ADAM
By Terri

The light on the phone machine blinked with an urgency, red flash against shiny plastic black. I couldn't ignore it. I didn't. I picked up the message from a client needing to speak to me right away about a young boy who had been injured in a terrible accident. I called her back. I listened with the ears of my heart, scanning every word she spoke as she described what had happened to Adam, and no, I had not heard of the story, and yes, I would consider it, and I told her it would take four days of prayer and contemplation to decide if I should take on this case.

I was unsure, unsettled. It was an amazing survival tale. I was not certain I could help, and clearly, I did not want to lead on the parents to any false hope. My employment working at a head injury clinic many years prior flashed before me…these were tough situations; what could I possibly have to offer?

By then I had combined a lifetime of clairvoyance with 25 years of meditating to guide people to the other side to where they needed to be; I liked to call myself "a midwife of many realms."

I have seen and sensed energy ever since I have a memory of being. I assumed as a child everyone did and also assumed it was a mutually skillful way to interact with reality. To receive another's thoughts in an intensity of light brings depth not gained by ordinary communication, to sense emotional tones through vivid colors, and to glean insight into intent is most helpful in developing personal interactions. By "seeing" I mean literally watching thought—forms around a person—or detecting emotions as colors flaring in synergistic waves. Sometimes I "hear" information—a word or phrase that prompts me to probe deeper. Occasionally an energetic story opens like an IMAX theater with detailed descriptions. It took years of empirical observation to understand what was happening and how reliable a tool it was. There came a point in my life when no longer could I deny the accuracy, even if it took time to unravel the meaning. Meditation has trained my mind to be calm. The midwifery practice is being with what is, as it is, without imposing anything onto the situation. Midwifery is the fierce and intimate knowing of life-force; the courage to protect, defend, and guide its righteous flow; and the willingness to be unafraid of the life/death/life pulse in every moment. Combined, these components of clairvoyance, meditation, and midwifery allow a process of moving through a situation into transformation, wherever or whatever that may be. Each event is unique; there are no set formulas I hold, just a willingness to share the profundity of such a journey. I have no soundbites for what I do; it is too layered.

It is delicate to do what I do in this highly technologic and skeptical culture. Often, it is misunderstood, maligned, or exploited. An intrinsic side of my work lies in the discernment of whether someone can actually receive my help. Is someone *willing* to receive? This is a necessary and vital question that must be answered before I take on a client. If someone is *not willing,* I am not interested. Part of the prayer and contemplation is the listening to whether there is receptivity to the journey. "I" am not the "doer"; it is a process, a relationship of transformation that is joined by the gifts cultivated in my life and shared with another. With each request, as I enter in contemplation and prayer, I place myself in the fullness of *not knowing,* and I wait, listen, and observe for an indication whether to proceed. I am only interested in the deepest possible healing in any given person or event, be it in the physical, mental, emotional, spiritual, or soul dimensions. The true nature of such healing requires us to change our minds and, in that process, be willing to be changed. Death, in this view, is never a failure, just a relocation of soul perception, and I am honored to join others in their transitions. Sorting out the receptivity, the needs, the requirements to fulfill the deepest healing, all this is brought as a continuum to the time of contemplation and prayer.

So, the prayer and contemplation for Adam began. Each morning I would meditate and ask if it was correct to take on this case. Each morning I heard nothing.

On the morning of the fourth day I left for an appointment in town, annoyed at myself, realizing I had forgotten an umbrella. The rain was heavy at times, and the dirt road that led from my house to the main road was rutted and muddy. As I approached the main road, about four or five yards from the intersection, I saw something on the ground. With a wet, foggy windshield, I wasn't sure. I stopped and got out. From behind, it looked like an owl, or maybe a hawk, and very dead, wings splayed on packed dirt and stones. I went back to the car and got some tobacco to make an offering to the spirit of the bird. I crept close and hunkered down, sprinkling the soft grains of tobacco, watching them float to the ground, and as I did, the bird swiveled around with a fierce, fast swoop. It stood upright and gathered in its wings. We were literally eye-to-eye, and neither of us blinked. I asked from my heart-mind: *Are you okay? What happened? How can I help you?*

The bird had a wide-eyed stare with a deep intensity that sent shudders through me. It did not move. I stood. The traffic on the intersecting road was busy. Often, people drove down this county two-lane like a highway, even in this wet weather. I took a few steps toward the road, thinking, *What to do? How to help?* I put out a prayer from the depths of my heart for help. As the rain pelted me, standing a few feet from the bird, I was now scared that if a car tried to turn in, it would flatten the bird. I placed myself immediately at the juncture of the two roads, praying, sometimes out loud, for help. A truck stopped; it was a yellow pickup truck with an MDC sign on the door. A man in a flannel shirt and jeans put a jacket over his head as he made his way to me.

"What we got here?" he asked.

"Don't know," I replied. "I just came upon it a few minutes ago, and didn't know what to do." I explained how I had found the bird and how it had moved quickly upright as I approached.

"I'm the raptor rehab specialist from the MDC," he said as he squatted down and looked intently at the bird.

He stood up and walked around the bird.

"Well," he said, "don't see any blood. And the fact that it has its wings folded up means that they are not broken….It is a juvenile red tail hawk. Must have been on a trial hunt and got its bearings mixed up. You know teenagers are like that. In a heartbeat they can get themselves into situations that are way over their heads….Probably chasing prey and bounced off a windshield."

He took off his jacket and threw it over the bird.

"You got time? To do some monitoring? I mean, can you stay and watch the bird? Make sure it is okay? I will give you my card, and you can call me. It is in shock, and when that wears off it should fly away. If not, well, call me; more serious injuries may have happened."

He proceeded to move the hooded bird gently to the side of the road and placed it on a branch lying on the roadside weeds, and then he carefully lifted his jacket as he handed me his card and said, "Well, I'm really on another call. Good luck!"

I turned and faced the bird, squatting eye-to-eye again, my feet wide and back rounded as rain rolled down the curve of my spine into puddles on the ground.

There was something about the eyes. So wide, unearthly in a way that I told myself it must be the shock. So deep those eyes, like it was telling me a story in a language I couldn't quite grasp. I trembled, so close to something this wild. The bird did not move.

After three hours, cramped and stiff, I needed to finally get to town.

"I'll be back," I whispered, "and, well, I hope you aren't here then."

A few hours later, I did return and the bird was gone. A thrill went through my heart.

The next morning I called the Dzialos and said yes. I would come and meet them.

I pulled up a steep driveway to a modest house on a hill. I was welcomed at the door by Sharon. We sat in the living room as she and Phil told me the story. I scanned them for the inevitable presence of shock. Shock, yes, and I sensed that they already had been beaten up by the process, a kind of "black and blue" pummeling in their energy fields. I noticed my own acute sensitivity to this, and I felt discomfort. I scanned for more about this, but clearly, the import of the story and Adam was central. I refocused my listening and scanned as they recounted the events, my inner eye seeing flashes of detail, the complex scenario with so many people involved.

They both were perched on the edge of the couch across from me, their spines lifted up and out of their pelvises like they were hung from an invisible hook that kept them in a watchful, tense uprightness. This was a kind of forced upright composure pushing them forward. I had seen this before. There are several ways of responding to shock and trauma; one end of the spectrum is to "fall apart" emotionally, another end to become overly efficient, and I wondered where they fell, now having taken

Adam out of the long-term care facility and being completely responsible for his care. They never asked for care for themselves, only Adam. They also had never met a "clairvoyant" before and were only contacting me at the urging of a good friend and because they had nowhere else to turn.

I nodded.

"Honestly, I don't know what I can do to help. I would like to meet Adam."

I was ushered into an adjoining room. Adam was in a reclining position in a hospital bed. His mouth was open, and his eyes, his eyes were wide and had a faraway, unearthly look.

They were identical in feeling to the hawk's eyes the day before. I moved closer. The same stare, the same deep intensity, the same whisper in a language I couldn't grasp.

Then I noticed a light…a small blue-silver circular light hovering in the corner of the room. I recognized the light. I knew exactly what to do. I spent a few minutes silently communicating with it. I placed my hand on Adam's heart as I spoke to his parents.

"His spirit is not in his body," I began. "Adam has not decided if he wants to live or die. It is important for his spirit to return to his body no matter what happens, because the shock of this and the dislocation of his spirit are grave. He cannot live with any quality of life without his spirit in his body, and he cannot die in peace with it detached from his body either."

I described a simple process of inviting his spirit back into his body. I communicated to him that I understood he had not decided. He did not move, his eyes held in a steady intensity.

His parents gave permission to me to invite his spirit back. Not wanting to plunge the parents into an overload of information or unfamiliar terrain in energetic and spiritual healing, I kept my hands on Adam's heart and silently invoked an intent communicating with his spirit, showing him exactly what I wanted to do and why, and proceeded to energetically merge with what I call "the secret chamber" of the heart. This energetic "space" of the heart is where I see the full unity of our heart, mind, and spirit. If this place is injured, separated, insulted, or disturbed in any way, there are serious consequences for the quality of life. Once contact was made, I opened energetic pathways to anchor his spirit back in. It only took a few minutes.

Sharon asked, "How do you know his spirit was *not* in his body?"

I replied, looking down and hesitating for a moment, remembering these people had no experience with such things, "Ah, well, actually, I can see it. It is hovering up there, in the corner of the ceiling." I motioned to the point above and behind them.

I gave Phil and Sharon a simple explanation of the secret chamber of the heart and how they could over the next few days place their hands on his heart like I did and invite Adam back into his body. They understood it was Adam's decision; even if his spirit returned, it was no guarantee of anything. As a colleague from the head clinic had reminded me, "Kids like this, after an injury like that, they just up and die with no explanation."

Only Adam could choose to live fully within this journey, or die; we would have to wait and see.

"Let's stay in touch," I said. "Adam will lead us in this."

Sharon called a few days later to report Adam slept more deeply since being released from the hospital. She also said that he wouldn't take his eyes off that corner where his spirit had been for three whole days, and that she and Phil would have to physically turn his head to straighten his gaze forward.

"I can feel something has shifted, let's keep going."

"Yes," is all I remember saying in reply. "Let's keep going."

SMILE

A child's first smile—what mother doesn't remember that moment? She tucks it gently away into her memory bank. She'll remember how she felt as she gazed into the sweetness of that smile. Then that smile will flow into the next—a natural and powerful energy filling this tiny being.

Adam lost his smile. It vanished on July 24, 1998—the day his body was pulled beneath the strong current of the river. No smile, no laugh, no light. He seemed stuck in blankness or pain and distress.

It was the second Christmas after his accident. The holidays felt so heavy. We maintained some of our family rituals for the sake of our daughter, Aimee. She tenaciously held on to "what used to be," demanding that we keep her life "like all of her friends." We decorated a beautiful tree, draping it in blue lights—a color we found soothing and warm. And then I prayed. I knew what I could not give Adam for Christmas—a new bike, snowboard, skis, skates, video game system, or four wheeler. I had to find something meaningful for my beautiful, silent, seriously injured boy. I prayed for something very simple. I asked for a smile—something beyond a "painful presence."

Apart from us, his aides and therapists, and a few visitors, Adam's only companion was the TV. One of his therapists told me emphatically to not allow Adam to wander off (stare at nothing—the walls, ceiling, into the nothingness of space), so when Adam was not engaged with a person, we would focus him on the TV, often physically moving his head toward the box, even if it was only to watch colors and shapes.

One particular day, the TV was tuned in to the news. Adam was watching; honestly, at this point, I never knew what he was consciously taking in. The sports news came on, and there was a clip about a violent act committed by a hockey player. This player had raised his stick above his head and forcefully flung it down onto another player's head. The other player was, thankfully, protected by a helmet, but it was nonetheless a traumatic and horrendously unsportsmanlike action. My son watched the incident and laughed out loud! He actually laughed with sound and laughed with his whole body. Given that my son had been a passionate hockey player at the young age of 12, with lots of testosterone flowing through his veins, on a very coarse, basic level, his reaction made perfect sense. For a brief moment, I wanted to scream at him, "Adam, that is so inappropriate to laugh at that!" Of course then the enormity of the moment struck me, and I wept. My prayer had been answered; I just had no control over the circumstances.

Throughout the day, this particular event was replayed many times. Each time, Adam's reaction was the same. He laughed. Part of it seemed so irreverent, laughing at someone's cruelty, yet it spoke volumes. Adam was more cognitively aware than anyone had given him credit for, and he was on his way back. He was breaking through, not in the prettiest fashion, but fairly typical for a 13-year-old boy.

I gently tucked this away into my memory bank.

THE RIVER

How do you move beyond a catastrophic event? Time, everyone says. I was not satisfied with that response. I had an intuitive feeling that we needed to go back to the river. Three years had passed since Adam's near-drowning. He was now 15 years old. Adam was attending my husband's school; this was the only way I could assure his safety. He was severely brain-injured, tube-fed, in a wheelchair. He was placed in a program for children with severe special needs, and he had Jody, a wonderfully compassionate one-to-one aide who acted like a second mother. Adam needed serious, loving, care-taking. Our daughter, Aimee, now 17, was completing her junior year in high school. I had returned to my job as a high school counselor.

With help and guidance from friends, we planned a ceremony at the site of the accident. I was prepared for an emotional day, but I could never have predicted the impact of that day on my daughter.

Aimee sat with us in our living room the morning before the ceremony. Aimee's life as she knew it had come to a screeching halt after her brother's accident. He was severely brain-injured and needed 24-hour care. She handled this with a mixture of anger, disappointment, frustration, and worry. Aimee had held on to her own life with incredible determination; her life was not going to change. She wanted her parents available, our finances solid, and, more than anything, she did not want to feel different from her friends. Aimee consistently challenged the premise that our life could never be the same again.

Our dear friends Terri and Jenny joined us for a quiet prayerful moment before we departed for the river. Terri had created the ceremony and would be facilitating the whole process. We were meeting a large gathering of friends, a few family members, therapists (old and new), and some staff members from the camp. The two counselors who had been supervising the boys the day of the incident had agreed to join us.

To Aimee, our bright, beautiful, tenacious daughter, almost everything and everyone we had invited into our lives since that day appeared bizarre: the therapies, the alternative medicines, the spiritual practices.

"Can't you just be normal? Can't you act like you used to? Why do you keep bringing strange people into our life? Isn't there any other way to do this?"

I tried to understand her feelings. Prior to this life-changing event, my husband and I had not been aware or open to these healing ways. Aimee's continual resistance troubled me immensely. I did not want to lose our daughter while we worked so hard to save our son.

Aimee invited two friends to join her for the river event. She refused to drive with us. She had chosen friends who might not judge whatever happened at the river that day. In other words, she felt safe with them.

We arrived at the home of one of Adam's therapists who coincidentally lived very close to the site of the accident. People gathered slowly in front of the house, each one taking a moment to greet our family. Eventually, we formed a huge circle to begin the first part of the planned ceremony. Aimee held back, probably wondering what kind of religion we had converted to—the blessings to the four directions, the prayers, and the burning of sage. I concentrated on the ceremony, pleading for some sense of peace in our life.

The group proceeded toward the river, singing a song written just for our celebration and gifted to us.

> River, touch our lives today.
> River, touch our lives today.
> Touch the anger and the fears, the guilt and the tears.
> River, touch our lives today.
> River, take them all away.
> River, take them all away.
> Take the anger and the fears, the guilt and the tears.
> River, take them all away.
> River, bring us love today.
> River, bring us love today.
> Bring the healing and the balm, the peace and the calm.
> River, bring us love today.

Aimee ran to the river, impatient with the procession, not willing to sing. She stumbled down the steep and rocky slope. We had never wanted her to face the scene of the accident alone. It had taken me three years to visit this place, and I had been accompanied by a therapist. Facing the scene, visualizing the accident, had been an overwhelming emotional experience for me. Aimee had no idea what she was about to experience. With the exception of the initial days and weeks following Adam's accident, she had never allowed herself to feel. If she felt sad, bad, or anxious, she could not function, and then she would not feel normal, a condition she would find intolerable. She therefore avoided feeling. Somehow, her stubborn, adolescent mentality worked this out for her. This day, however, would be different.

When we reached the path that would lead us to the site, we were initially preoccupied with Adam. He had been in his wheelchair during the procession, but now he needed to be carried down the rocky, steep hill and held by the river for the second part of the ceremony. We had baskets of flower petals, each basket symbolizing a different emotion—anger, fear, guilt, and sadness. Phil and I awkwardly held Adam, his rigid body not easily conforming to sitting in front of us close to the shore and not far from the rock that had entrapped his foot nearly three years ago. I held on tight and watched as all of the participants walked in front of us, gathered petals from the four baskets, and offered them to the river with a blessing.

After some time had passed, I began to search for my daughter. I found her standing away from the group, sobbing intensely. I left Adam with my husband and gathered her into my arms.

"Mom, I hate this; I just want to leave. All of these people are weird. This whole day has been awful. I don't want to do this."

A bouquet of flowers had been set aside for our family, the same type of flowers used in the ceremonial baskets. I gathered them, took Aimee by the hand and brought her to the river's edge, and said through my tears, "This is how you can make peace with the river, the accident, and the huge changes in your life. This is what you can do because you miss your brother. Take these flowers—your anger, your fear, your guilt, and your sadness—and offer them to the river. The river never meant us harm. The river held your brother and brought him back to us."

With my arms around her, I watched as Aimee gently tossed the flowers, one by one, into the rushing waters. For one moment, one beautiful moment, Aimee joined us, no resistance. She allowed herself to participate in not only her brother's healing but also her own.

JOHREI AND FATHER SPIRIT

Terri was encouraging us to be open to gentle, deep, non-invasive forms of healing. As I let go of one traditional therapy after another, we were finding room in our life for this level of healing. One weekend, we set out to track down a new therapy. We found it in an unremarkable ranch house in a wooded residential neighborhood. There was no sign—just the right number for the Sunbow 5 Foundation. I held my breath, something I did not necessarily find helpful but that was my natural reaction to new people. We unloaded Adam from our van and entered the side door of the house. Immediately, we were greeted at the door by a group of Japanese men and women. They asked us to remove our shoes at the door and then guided us into a large, sparsely furnished room. There were chairs and a vase filled with flowers. A framed Japanese character was the only wall adornment.

All I knew at this point, from information shared by Terri, our ever-present guide, was that this community of people had dedicated their lives to offering a very powerful healing method called Johrei. With this simplistic introduction, we entered new territory. The translator, Naoko, explained that we would first receive Johrei and then we would sit together and talk. One man and two women immediately surrounded Adam; Phil and I were asked to sit across from another man and woman who would offer us Johrei individually. We were told to just sit, relax, and close our eyes. Each giver extended his or her right arm and intensely focused on channeling divine light through him- or herself to us. I sat in the chair, grateful for the reprieve. Someone was taking care of Adam, and I could rest, quiet my mind, and receive.

After the first session, we talked for a long time about Adam's accident. Every detail seemed important to their understanding about what might be necessary from their perspective to help with our son's healing. They also taught us about Johrei. They explained that they offer Johrei as an instrument of healing and spiritual awakening. I was sitting and thinking, *My God, have I not been awakened enough?* We were encouraged to think deeply about our ancestors. What "spiritual clouds" might have been passed along to us by the actions of our ancestors? I had many thoughts about this question. Was my son paying for the actions of our ancestors? Who was responsible—my family or Phil's? How would we ever know? How could this be helpful to my nonverbal, wheelchair-bound son?

Because I had made a commitment to leave no stone unturned when it came to finding ways for my son to heal, I decided to enter their world. For over a year, we would visit Sunbow 5 on most weekends. At a time when my family and our community had ceased to be a presence in our life, the attention, compassion, and hope for healing that we received from this community of Japanese healers was most welcome.

At some point, when they believed that Adam needed much more Johrei than they could offer, we were invited to go through a training. They were anxious to see more tangible signs of Adam's healing. We were taught about the basic philosophy that underlies the practice of Johrei, much of it based on the Shinto religion. We took it all in, anxious as always to find ways to be helpful to Adam and ourselves by embracing anything that would bring meaning and understanding into our new reality. We received the Ohikari, a gold medallion that encased a seal with the Japanese character for "light" written on it. This medallion would allow us to give Johrei to Adam—we would be empowered. Naoko, one of the women whom I came to trust and admire for her sincerity and deep intuitive abilities, carefully explained that, because we were Adam's parents, our unconditional love for him made any Johrei that he received from us very powerful. We worked on our own for months, returning to the Foundation a few times for small gatherings.

One weekend, Naoko called to let us know that it was time to discuss those potential spiritual clouds. She believed that something very deep was impacting—interfering with—Adam's healing. So, Phil and I went to work, exploring whose ancestors could be meddling. Everything kept pointing to my side of the family, primarily my father. This did not make me happy. As a matter of fact, I felt burdened by this realization. I sat with it for a time and then declared, "Whatever it takes."

Exactly 40 years before my son's near-drowning accident, my father was involved in a car accident in the middle of the night while on a fishing trip with my grandfather and uncle. He had broken his neck, dying a short while later. He was 40 years old, father of five children, and a pharmacist who owned his own business. He worked too hard and rarely rested. Family and relatives had clearly been worried about him (though I was too young at the time to be aware of this). The circumstances of his death, though explained as a car accident, were somewhat muddled. He self-medicated—quite easy for a pharmacist—and may not have been in a clear state of mind the night of the accident. Only he knew for certain what actually happened that night. This was an "unresolved" death and, according to the Johrei community, warrants a huge spiritual cloud.

Our Japanese friends explained to us that Adam's survival could be connected to this father spirit—righting a wrong, making an apology to a daughter or the calming of an unsettled spirit. Something had happened in that moment at the river when Adam struggled between life and death—a spirit entered our world, easing our son back to life and to a long, labored recovery. My father, given that the circumstances of his death were unresolved, may have been waiting in that place and time, waiting for an opportunity to move beyond his death toward spiritual peace. He was not at peace and our son's accident provided an opportunity. He aligned himself that day with my son's spirit and for several years had been sharing Adam's healing. Our task at this point was to coax my father's spirit away from Adam and to help my father move on to a new place. The Johrei community, through ritual and ceremony, would assist us.

A ONE-OF-A-KIND
FAMILY REUNION

How? Where? I kept wondering what the Johrei folks meant—connect with my father spirit and coax him to a new place? I was told that I needed to go to my father's gravesite and there a ceremony would be performed. And this all must happen soon.

I had not visited my birthplace, Springville, New York for more than 25 years. We moved away when I was 10 years old, my mother newly remarried and my stepfather wanting to work in New York City. Returning to this place seemed like a daunting task. I no longer had family in the area, at least none that I knew about or maintained contact with. I needed to find the location of the cemetery and then the actual gravesite. My childhood memory had not stored this information even though I remembered attending the funeral.

I decided to make an initial trip by myself. Our Japanese friends fully intended to accompany me to my father's gravesite. They believed in their power to initiate a ceremony to connect with the father spirit; they had the tools. I have to admit that I was baffled by this group's selflessness. The winter season had just begun, and this area of New York is well-known for difficult winters and intense snowfall. It would be an eight-hour car ride from our home in Massachusetts. Given that I did not want these folks to waste any time while I wandered around, I set off to do the preliminary work.

Leaving home, as always, was no small feat. I had to make sure that Adam had everything he needed and that Phil would have enough help while I was away. Suffice it to say, Philip was very supportive of this journey. Hey, he did not have to go, nor did he have to connect with a dead person!

I left feeling anxious about the weather. Snow was in the forecast. It was the beginning of December 2002. Driving was smooth until I hit Buffalo, New York. Springville was within an hour of this city. As I drove closer to my destination, I actually experienced a complete white-out. I did not know what to do—no visibility whatsoever. I could not pull over; I could not stop; I could not see behind me or in front of me. I was terrified. I just kept moving and talking and talking. I had one of those infamous conversations with God: "I'm in your hands now. Please don't let me down." After a very long half hour, I reached the exit, found the hotel, and collapsed into a deep, exhausted sleep.

The next morning, the snow continued falling, but no white-out conditions were predicted, just a steady, wet downfall. Armed with directions and covered in snow gear, I set out to find the site. I arrived at the cemetery, immediately struck by the magnitude of my task. The cemetery was huge, and many of the gravestones were covered in snow. Town records had given me the exact location of the site, but I could not find my bearings. I walked around aimlessly, brushing snow off many, many stones. I was soaking wet by now, cold and frustrated, angry and deflated. I pictured myself, in that moment, crumpling down into the snow and just letting go. I did not do this. Instead, I began to head back toward the car, thinking that I would go back into town and solicit some help. I was muttering all the way: "Look, God, I have come a long way. I have an important job, and I need some help." I stopped for a moment and noticed one gravestone that seemed to be commanding my attention. The name was clear—Gerald Kuhn, my father's brother. He, too, had died an early death. I scouted around the nearby graves, apologizing to God for my doubting thoughts. I frantically brushed the snow off the nearby stones until I found it—Edwin P. Kuhn, my father. This time I buckled down into the snow on my knees. I was talking and crying at the same time, still wet and cold but completely lost in this moment, this magnificent reunion. Even though I had only been eight years old at the time of my father's death, I missed him. Something always felt unfinished. He had died in the middle of the night, and I had never really said good-bye.

Earlier in the day, I purchased a tiny Christmas tree intending to place it by my father's stone – a marker for my next trip. It was more than that. I explained to my father what I needed, what my son needed, and left the tree as a gift and a reminder.

I returned home and waited for direction regarding our next step which appeared to be a group trip to the gravesite. However, the snow storms had intensified in New York State and travel was out of the question. We would, instead, have the ceremony in our Greenfield living room. I was grateful about this turn of events; now Phil and Adam would be with me.

On the arranged day I paced, peered through the windows and nervously moved around chairs, tables, and Adam. I had been instructed to set up a ceremonial table with flowers, food, trinkets, and wine, all commemorating my father. I had spent days digging through boxes of old pictures, exploring memories. I remembered that my father had always worn a bowtie, his trademark of professionalism. He smoked a pipe; he peeled raw potatoes and ate them like apples. I found two pictures to place on the altar. One was a very handsome portrait of my father; the other was a small snapshot of me in a frilly, puffy pink dress sitting on my father's lap in his favorite chair. His arms encircled me. Beside the photos on the table I placed a plate of food – all German fare.

Finally, the Japanese contingent arrived, bearing more flowers, saki, costumes, and musical instruments for the ceremony. The men excused themselves to change into brown robes, and Mineko, an enchanting, soulful woman, arrived in full ceremonial garb, reminiscent of a Geisha without the pancake makeup. Mineko was the mistress of the ceremony. Phil and I were mesmerized, never imagining how anything this elaborate and beautiful could be happening for us. The group carefully examined my thoughtful preparations and were pleased. We were ready to proceed.

Sprigs of evergreen had been prepared by one of the men, and I, as daughter to this father, was to make the first offering. I was told to place the sprig on the altar and then clap three times. These directions were given by the translator, Naoko, and through example. I have to admit that I was suffering from performance anxiety. What if I didn't place the evergreen on the table correctly or clap at the right time or in the right way? Some may wonder why I followed this Johrei practice with such seemingly blind faith. Was I playing the role of desperate mother willing to listen, to believe in anything and anyone who offered hope and change? Was this the magic we needed? I can honestly say that these folks walked their talk. They wanted to help us, whatever that meant. I admired and benefited from their immense altruism. Also, the explanations they offered us based on their core beliefs about this life often resonated deeply for both Phil and me. We were trying hard to make sense out of our life events and to help Adam.

The entire ceremony lasted about 15 minutes. The instrumental music, based on the most ancient classical music of Japan, to my Americanized ears, was coarse and hardly melodious. We stood in a group, Phil and I with Adam in his wheelchair between us. We listened to the Japanese prayers. I eventually stepped forward to make my offering, placing the sprig directly in front of my father's picture. I felt his presence deeply, this recent immersion beginning with the trip to his gravesite and concluding with my preparations for the ceremonial table, the memories of an eight-year-old child translated into the consciousness of a 52-year-old woman. I moved away from the table and clapped three times; Adam jumped after each clap, his sensitive nervous system startled by the sudden loudness.

We exchanged pleasantries with the group, and then Naoko sat with me and detailed my new responsibility. For the next year, I must consciously and daily honor my father. I was to set up a small altar, light a candle, and keep his picture in view. Each time we had a special dinner, I was to place a small offering on the altar. She said, "You must connect with him through active practice for the entire year."

I was faithful, conscientious, and, at times, lighthearted about this practice. I never questioned. I just followed. If this was what it would take to coax my father away from my son, to free him so Adam would not have to share his healing with my father, then I had no questions. I followed the directions perfectly.

Exactly one year later, we repeated a much simpler ceremony. This time we were basically terminating the connection, resolving the spiritual cloud. A channeled message was offered to me from my father:

> "Thank you very much for today's ceremony.
> From now on, I will begin my own training and promise that I will not cause further troubles to the physical world.
> I sincerely thank you again.
> I am grateful to Sharon and Phil.
> With regard to Adam, due to the karma from his and my previous lives, Adam has to go through this suffering.
> I am sorry about what happened to him.
> I will clear up this karma and then leave from him.
> I must go now."

MY DEPOSITION

Out of absolute necessity, we filed a lawsuit two years after the accident. Though taking care of our body-mind-spirit issues was critically important, we needed, at the same time, to be vigilant and proactive regarding our everyday practical concerns. While I managed all care and therapy for Adam, Phil was taking charge of our family's future, attempting to ensure that our son would have what he needed for his rehabilitation in the present and the future. He was also seeking justice, believing that many neglectful actions had led to Adam's accident. It was a long and arduous process, and it was not until the fifth year after the accident that we were even ready for the depositions.

This was my moment of truth. I was scheduled to give my deposition. I thought I was prepared. Most of the other depositions were completed. I had attended many of them, naively thinking that I would finally have an opportunity to hear the true story of the accident. Everyone, under oath, must tell the truth, the whole truth, and nothing but the truth, right? I came to realize that people told "their truth" but it was nothing that brought us any resolution or peace. It was so easy to say, "I don't remember. It happened so long ago." Those folks were prepped to only answer questions, to never offer more. Defensive posturing was the norm. Don't admit any liability. Don't acknowledge any guilt. Never offer an apology or gesture of sympathy.

All had been counseled not to have any contact with us or they would risk their livelihoods and reputations.

The other depositions had been given in our hometown. My husband and I had to travel to Springfield to a large bank in a cold and impersonal conference room. I entered the room with intense trepidation. Today was my day. I wanted an opportunity to tell my story under oath, but I realized that I had no control over the questions. I sat with my attorney across the table from the state's attorney. The questions began, one after another—no time to breathe, no time to collect my thoughts, no time to quiet my pounding heart.

"Did you find the camp? How much research had you done? What kind of student was Adam? Did Adam have any behavioral issues? Had he taken swimming lessons? What sports did he participate in?"

The lawyer's tactic was becoming increasingly clear. Here was a mother who had enrolled her son in a camp, with full knowledge of the activities and the liabilities involved. The son was a high-energy athletic boy who may not have been listening to the counselor's instructions on the day of the river accident.

As the battering questions continued, I felt myself becoming increasingly defensive. I kept thinking, *Wait a minute! I was not at the river that day. No mention of the river activity ever appeared in the schedule or any brochure. How can anyone hold me responsible? And, my son, he was 12 years old and placed in a treacherous situation. How could anyone hold him responsible?*

I was so weary. I was absolutely unprepared for the ruthless direction my deposition was taking. The assistant attorney general, who represented the college, shuffled some papers and then looked directly at me. He handed me the signed permission slip for the camp activities and pointed at my signature. I nodded. He then pointed at Adam's. I felt a direct hit to my solar plexus and doubled over. Enough. . . I stood up, fled the room, entered the hallway, and crumpled to the floor, weeping. Images of my son flooded my consciousness: Adam stopping hockey pucks with his glove and stick; Adam catching a ball at first base with his strong right arm; Adam throwing a soccer ball away from the net when he was playing goalie; Adam hugging me. Then I pictured my boy in his wheelchair with his contracted, immobile arms. I picked myself up, returned to the room, and sat back down at the table and stared into the young attorney's eyes. I said, "That was my son's signature when he was able to sign his name."

The rest of the day was a blur—I was feeling numb and in shock. I sat through my husband's deposition and, thankfully for him, he was not battered emotionally. We conferred with our attorney, who expressed nothing but disgust for the tactics employed by the opposition, calling it cruel and inhumane. We then drove home to Adam.

My uncontrollable tears began in earnest the next morning. I was home alone. Adam and Phil had left for school. I couldn't stop. What was it? Was I feeling embarrassed? Humiliated? Bruised and battered? It felt deeper, but I had yet to name it. I was getting nowhere, couldn't seem to gain any sense of control. I called Terri, and she said, "I will come to you, or you come here right now."

I walked into her house and into her arms. She threw a blanket around me and guided me to the fireplace. The constant sobbing had left me shivering uncontrollably. Terri gently encouraged me to let it all out. I cried until I literally had no more tears.

Then the work began. I slowly and painstakingly came to terms with my truth. As Adam's mother, I took his hand and guided him to an adventure that I thought would add to the quality of his life. I was responsible for getting Adam to the river. I found the camp. I filled out the paperwork. I spoke with the director of the camp on the phone. I signed the permission forms. Adam signed the forms in front of me. I drove him to the community college every day. I packed his bag for the overnight camp-out. I made sure that his bathing suit was in his bag.

I had trusted the camp and the college. I may not have been at the river on the day of the accident, but I was responsible for bringing this experience into his life. It was time to accept this. I sat with this reality, my reality. Over the next few days, I was able to name my darkness. It was guilt—raw, blinding, and intensely painful. I was drowning in guilt and grief. I sat with this and suffered until I finally came to the realization that I could move through it—accept my guilt, acknowledge my grief, and forgive myself.

SEDUCTION OF HOPE

Concurrent with the lawsuit, bankruptcy, work, deep and relentless fatigue, and isolation, we continued our search for the most effective approach to Adam's recovery. The path seemed to take us further and further away from the norm. The journey was not always smooth, and sometimes, our judgment was clouded by the complicated emotions surrounding a life-changing injury to a child. We were fragile and frightened, willing to latch on to any hint of hope. What follows is an example of things not always being what they appear to be. This non-traditional physical therapy practice was recommended to us by someone who had the best of intentions.

It was not the typical, austere clinical setting of most physical therapy practices. In the reception area, we were met with an immensely engaging welcome—heartfelt greetings, immediate connection with Adam, and reverent talk of God and his power. The sitting area was comfortable and tastefully decorated. I felt like I was being invited into a friend's living room. Another room was filled with videos, toys, and books for the children, like a friend's family room. Parents with children in wheelchairs, with walkers, and with feeding tubes patiently awaited their appointments. We introduced ourselves and exchanged our stories.

When we entered the treatment room, the light was dimmed and Christian music was playing softly in the background. It was church-like, quiet and peaceful. Andrew, the head therapist and owner of the practice, shook our hands, listened to a brief rendition of Adam's story to date, and immediately put his hands on Adam.

Adam was wearing knee-high splints from a recent tendon-release operation—an operation we had initially believed to be critical for Adam's recovery and comfort. Andrew questioned the purpose, removed the splints, and checked Adam over in a diagnostic fashion. While he was working, he questioned us about our religious affiliation. We politely explained that we were not connected to a religion but we were, indeed, connected to God. He said, "Oh, I thought that I saw an angel on the way into the room."

I startled when I heard his words and felt the impact in my gut. Angels are symbols of strength and support and had taken on a significant and compelling presence in my life during this time. People gave me statues and trinkets of angels, and I placed them everywhere, banishing away my fears. How had he known this about me, and did he really see angels? I let this go and stood in awe of this man. Who was he and what did he have to offer our son?

Eventually, Andrew looked at Phil and me and told us unequivocally that Adam was communicating with him, telling him that he wanted to walk and talk again. This was not the first time someone had come into our lives with this gift of communication. Andrew then stood Adam on his feet and moved Adam's legs to mimic a walk. I looked at Phil, and his eyes held the same tears of hope, joy, and relief.

We left that day as true believers. We had traveled two hours each way to bring Adam to this practice. We continued our relationship for four years, visiting once a month. Several times, we booked an intensive, which meant back-to-back appointments for three days in a row. The physical therapy practice included many kind and skilled therapists, though we worked primarily with the head therapist. The primary therapy offered by this clinic was called "manual therapy," which to me, a non-therapist, initially looked like craniosacral, a very gentle and deep method used to improve sensory, motor, and neurological functions, which were all seriously impaired in Adam. Gentle and deep—it appeared perfect.

Twice a year, the therapists and their families offered a week-long camp experience. For me it was a welcome distraction from isolation. To be surrounded by families who truly understood our life and our challenge was extremely comforting. Many therapists would donate their time so all of the children present at the camp would receive at least two treatment sessions a day. A large room was set up for treatment with six massage tables. It was not unusual to find at each table three therapists working on each child, a multi-hands approach. I was grateful for this unique opportunity, and I expressed it often.

I held the belief, at that time, that there was something very powerful about this practice. I found Andrew to be a charismatic man who inspired confidence in everyone he taught, employed, and treated. From my vantage point, Adam seemed to be one of the clients earmarked to be treated primarily by this man. I don't remember ever directly requesting this, and I wasn't sure that requests for particular therapists were even permitted. It felt like an honor. Was Adam special? I wondered if perhaps Andrew saw such potential in Adam that he really wanted to work with him. Adam could be his poster boy. Obviously, all of these thoughts were my projection, reading between the lines, searching for a miracle. Did Andrew have the answer? Did he know the way to bring Adam back to walking and talking? There were times when I fantasized about moving closer to this practice to get more treatment for Adam and to live in a community where it appeared that more people understood the challenges of a severely injured child. I was not able to look at this experience with a critical eye; I was a convert.

This unquestioned position slowly began to erode, however. There came a time when I wanted more communication between myself and Andrew. Adam was nonverbal; I needed Andrew's feedback, and he needed mine. I would hear perfunctory comments like, "Adam did great work today!" All I saw was Adam lying on a massage table. Additionally, because this practice mentored student physical therapists, a many-hands approach would be used and the head therapist would be teaching throughout the session. This never bothered me; the more the better, I thought. And I was hoping that I could learn something myself. Given that my hands were not on Adam, I just heard the spoken word and learned little. Most parents were encouraged not to be present during the sessions because the therapists were concerned that the "parent energy" might interfere with the process of the therapy. Parents were not to be seen or heard. I tearfully removed myself for a time, not wanting to be responsible for any blockage, and honestly reflected upon my emotional state. Yes, I was tired. Yes, I was impatient. Yes, I was protective. Yes, I was a mother.

Maribeth, a shiatsu therapist who worked with Adam weekly, accompanied me once when I was attempting to stay out of the sessions. Because she was a trained therapist with craniosacral experience, I saw no reason why she could not stay in the session and observe or participate, given Andrew's propensity to mentor students. He did allow Maribeth to stay, and I was relieved. I would have an eyewitness account of that particular session. A young woman was working with Andrew that day, and when the session was finished, she came to get me and informed me that the session had been very exciting. Adam, according to both Andrew and this young woman, had spoken their names. Now, I knew my beautiful son was nowhere near verbal; he barely vocalized at this point. I looked at Maribeth; her facial expression spoke volumes. She did not believe this, nor had she witnessed this as an observer. I have no idea what these two therapists heard during this session; I was left feeling flustered and confused. Maribeth was furious. I, however, wanted to believe and was not willing to walk away. I did, however, insert myself back into the sessions.

One final session convinced us that the overall philosophy of the practice and of Andrew in particular left something to be desired. My husband took Adam to his appointment that day, and it was a particularly intense session. The focus of the treatment for Adam had changed over the four years. The gentle approach had been replaced by something more invasive. Using a traditional osteopathic model, the work had moved into myofascial release, joint mobilization, and manipulation. Andrew was a very strong muscular man, and he handled Adam with ease, lifting him, setting him on a ball, shifting him from side to side. I was amazed by his physical prowess. When Adam had sessions like this, it was not unusual for him to vomit, and I would still hear comments like, "Adam came to work today" and "He did great!" I kept quiet during most sessions because I thought that I needed to allow the therapist to concentrate, to not lose focus. I also did not want to be asked to leave. On this day, once Phil got Adam back in his wheelchair and strapped in the van, Adam moaned all the way home, making a horrific two hours for his father watching helplessly in the rear view mirror as his son sat in the back in obvious pain.

Adam suffered for several days, and we did not understand the root of the pain. My husband was livid. He would not tolerate anyone hurting his son. Andrew would not speak to me on the phone but wanted us to return for another session, which meant a two-hour drive with a very unhappy, uncomfortable boy. I was so confused. How could something that seemed to embrace everything we thought we needed for Adam and ourselves feel so wrong now? I had to look beyond the potential community, beyond the charismatic leader, beyond the good intention. Obviously, Andrew felt that "some pain" was necessary in Adam's process of recovery and, most importantly, that he had no need to explain himself. We never returned, and they never called to find out why.

My husband and I began to recognize in ourselves the "seduction of hope" that many families experience when they find themselves in desperate situations. If you tell them that their disabled sons will walk and talk again, they believe you. If you tell them that more is better, they will sell some of their prized possessions or beg and borrow to make this happen. We were just too vulnerable, too tired, and too afraid. We lost our censoring abilities. Discernment was beyond our reach. Gullible, yes. Looking for a miracle, yes. We are grateful that only some of our therapeutic experiences held this kind of conflict. As we recovered from our deep shock and learned to take better care of ourselves, we regained our footing and were able to see people as they are and to find those who could authentically add something to the quality of our son's life, though this process of discernment continues to be challenging.

ABR

I had retired from my job as a high school counselor, so with more available time and energy, I searched for new possibilities for Adam. We explored hyperbaric oxygen, neuro-biofeedback, chiropractic, integrated body awareness, always looking for ways to help Adam become more comfortable in his body. As a result of his brain injury, Adam had suffered severe musculoskeletal collapse. He had scoliosis and contractures in both upper and lower extremities. He was unable to use his arms and legs. We had removed Adam's feeding tube at the three-year mark, and he was making steady progress with eating and drinking.

While surfing the internet, I discovered a fascinating new approach to brain injury. It was called Advanced Bio-mechanical Rehabilitation (ABR); I immediately saw possibility and, potentially, the missing piece to the puzzle for Adam's long-term recovery. ABR redefines rehabilitation for the brain-injured. Everything I read about this new philosophy made perfect sense to me, despite my lack of background in anatomy and physiology and, more importantly, biomechanics. Leonid Blyum, the inventor of ABR, has developed a unique biomechanically based rehabilitation approach for children and young adults with brain injury that promises a predictable recovery of the musculoskeletal structure and motor functions. Most significantly, the parents are trained to perform the hands-on method of manual applications to their child's body. No more travel to therapists! We were to become our own child's therapists. I recognized a dramatic new way of thinking. The techniques themselves are gentle and deep. Adam's path to recovery encompassed these ingredients. Trauma is deep and multi-layered. We were willing and able to jump on board, to be pioneers. We contacted the ABR Center, which was located in Montreal, Quebec, and within a month, we had begun our new adventure.

For the first three years, we were required to report for training four times each year. This was our 12th trip. We compressed the trip into four days, and I found myself feeling compressed—breathe, breathe, breathe. . . .

Five hours of driving—one stop for food and gas and one stop at the border, where we had to repeatedly explain the intent of our visit. We explained that we must travel to Montreal to receive treatment for our injured son because he could not get anything comparable in the United States. The border guards seemed interested only in contraband and terrorists. They saw my son in his wheelchair and quickly sent us on our way.

We entered downtown Montreal, found our hotel, unloaded our van full of food, supplies, and clothes. We can never travel lightly. Adam's needs necessitate a multiplicity of items. We are in survival mode. A quick change and a bit of food, and we rushed to the center, where Adam was evaluated for an hour and a half.

The Montreal Center is administered by Annie, also a parent of a severely disabled boy. She is one of us and so much more. Not only does she understand and live our challenge but she has positioned herself to help other parents. Without her, this new therapy would not be readily available for parents in North and South America. ABR is a worldwide initiative, and Leonid, the inventor, travels extensively to many other centers.

During the evaluation, we removed Adam's clothes, and he laid on a flat table under the lights. The sessions were video-taped and photographed. Leonid gently perused Adam's long, thin body and explored the dynamic changes in his physical landscape. Yes, yes, yes—three big releases. Adam's musculoskeletal structure was moving in the right direction, away from the collapse. The quality of his skin had changed dramatically, a necessary stepping stone in this long process of rehabilitation. These words were magical, and we received them with humble gratitude. Someone had embraced the depth of Adam's physiological trauma and offered us a realistic plan. We focused on each change systematically. Leonid often tells us that he is not a psychic and cannot predict Adam's future, only promise continued improvement and change. And because we parents deliver the treatment, we are empowered to change our children's lives and help re-sculpt their bodies.

Once the evaluation was completed, we returned to the hotel and fell into an exhausted sleep. The next morning, we left the hotel only to be confronted with the bone-chillingly frigid Canadian air. The van started, thankfully, and we returned to the center for our first day of training. Over the next three days, we received five new exercises. Leonid examined each new bump on Adam's head—a depression here, increased volume there. During the next three months, we would be focusing on Adam's ear pit, his neck and shoulder separation, his clavicle, the triangle behind the sternocleidomastoid muscle, and the top of his head. We sat with an atlas of the human body and practiced each exercise. Adam was so tolerant. As long as he was positioned within viewing range of his DVD player, he rarely complained.

This trip promised an exciting addition to our program for Adam. Leonid invented a machine to help the ABR parents, complementing the manual exercises. Most of Adam's exercises are head and neck; the machine provides chest, abdomen, back, sacrum, and lateral pelvis coverage. Most families can manage three to four hours of therapy each day. With the machine, this time could be exponentially increased. The goal is faster and more consistent change.

We spent an afternoon with a woman from Singapore. Singapore was the first location to experiment with the machine about nine months before. Sarah had become the expert. She measured Adam's head and designed a temple exercise. My son looked like an alien, and I found myself holding my breath, waiting for him to rebel. Would he cough, laugh, growl, or tighten? He surprised me and instead allowed this intrusive, awkward headpiece to be plastered on his head. It consisted of bladders that were inflated and deflated by the machine, held in place with foam and Velcro belts. Sarah walked away after telling me to keep the headpiece on Adam to check his tolerance level.

My husband and Maribeth, the therapist who had accompanied us to Montreal, left to find some lunch. I looked at Adam and could not stop laughing. I needed to feed him lunch while he was wearing this contraption. He was not happy. He began to cough, complain, and holler. Somehow, I managed to feed him lunch, but his eyes spoke volumes. I quickly made the decision that I would never compromise his mealtime; no machine, just eating—pure and simple. I was exhausted at the end of this day.

We showed up for the last day, which was the last training and a check-in on the machine. We are a great team; the center recognizes us as Team Adam. I took copious notes and mapped the construction of each exercise. Phil photographed the setups, and Maribeth performed the exercise. Many families enlist extra help with ABR, apart from both parents; the more hands, the better. We were extremely fortunate to have found someone like Maribeth to help us. Each one of us has a defined role on the team. And Adam, as always, is the receiver.

We finished by noon, chatted with a few families, and bid farewell to the center staff until spring. The drive home was uneventful until we hit the border. Cars were being pulled over and searched. We waited in line and were too tired to be patient. We finally reached the gate, handed over our passports, and, within seconds, were allowed to pass. Evidently, we did not look suspicious.

The next morning, I awakened, sent my son off to school, stared at the packed suitcases and supplies, and walked out the door. I needed to decompress, and then I could organize everything that we had learned, make the necessary changes to our routine, and move forward—one building block at a time.

DISSONANCE

I was determined to talk with Mary, our son's physical therapist. She entered our living room ready to work with Adam. The equipment was set up—a variety of huge balls placed in the middle of the rug. Adam would be lifted onto these balls or be draped over them as Mary gently encouraged his body to stretch and open. I always acted as the assistant. Adam was long, lean, and very spastic, not an easy combination to work with.

This therapist had worked with Adam for more than six years, at least twice a week, sometimes more. She rarely missed an appointment, and she was always on time. She was strong and committed. When Adam returned to school two years after his accident, she even met him there to give him treatment sessions.

This time, I asked her to sit on the couch with me; Adam's session could wait. We had been involved in the new therapy, ABR, for quite some time. It was labor intensive; the more hands the better. I was prepared to ask her to join us in this new therapy. At first, I had believed that physical therapy and ABR would complement each other, but this was not the case. Stretching contracted muscles, standing on contracted feet, and kneeling on rigid knees were contraindicated by ABR. We were at a juncture.

I had become very fond of this woman. Mary was a mother and a gentle person. During the sessions, we often talked about my family, her family, and life experiences. I did not want to lose her in our life, and we needed help in the form of trained hands and familiarity with anatomy and physiology.

Prior to Mary's arrival that day, I had daydreamed about the many therapists who had come and gone from our life since Adam's accident. Given my fragile emotional state and my intense feelings of isolation in those early years, I had sometimes believed that these therapists who entered our life to work with Adam were my family. I needed these folks as much or more than Adam did. I did not want to be alone with this intense challenge, and it appeared that each and every one was agreeing to shoulder some of the responsibility. We entered a partnership. Unfortunately, I often lost perspective. Even though I had more than twenty years of experience as a counselor, I was unable to recognize and, at times, accept the boundaries of the therapeutic relationship or the transference that might be happening because I was grieving the loss of family and community. I encountered enormous turmoil when I needed to move Adam on to another therapy, the boundaries between therapist, friend, and family were all so blurred for me.

I sat facing Mary. My hands and voice were shaking. She listened politely. I had given her copies of Adam's evaluations in Montreal and had shared all of the available information. She had never reacted. It was her non-response that motivated me to have this conversation. I wondered if Mary thought we were making a mistake, undertaking this new therapy. I wondered if she had bothered to read the material. And I wondered if she was beginning to see that her work might not complement ABR. It did matter to me. I asked. She explained that the new therapy felt so dissonant with her own training that she could not, in good conscience, continue to work with us. She did not want to hurt Adam, and she was not willing or able to move away from her training to learn something new. We both ended up in tears, and I felt that I had lost a friend. She left us, and I grieved for a long time, missing her companionship. Mary never saw Adam again.

I couldn't help but tangle with the larger question. Had family and friends experienced the same dissonance? Were we making decisions and doing things that others could not reconcile with how they were choosing to live their own lives? Was this why we were so often alone? This journey, whether the search for the most effective treatment for brain recovery or the side trips that taught us time and again that Adam's healing and our own must incorporate body, mind, and spirit, was fraught with complicated relationships, conflict, and loss.

THE DAY OF WAILING

Adam's healing is beautiful, frightening, exciting, sad, joyful, and continually leaves us filled with anticipation, wondering, "What's next?"

Phil's phone call surprised me. He and Adam had left for school almost an hour before. All he said was, "Something is happening." I could hear Adam in the background and only one word came to my mind "wailing." My nonverbal son, who held his body so tight that his voice and vocalizations came out in strangulated tones, was loudly and openly wailing, nonstop.

I was aware of my husband's worried ranting. "What should I do? Should I call the doctor?"

Despite my immediate panic and fear, I knew only one thing. "Bring him home. He needs to be home."

Phil was in the nurse's office at the school, and neither he nor the nurse could see any physical reason for Adam's distress, so Phil did as I asked. He put Adam back in his wheelchair van and drove him home. Adam calmed during the trip. As Phil pulled up the driveway, I ran out of the house and flung open the van door, desperate to hold and soothe Adam.

Phil unlocked the chair and said, "When he sees you he will cry—trust me." At that moment, Adam caught my eyes and the wailing began. His eyes were filled with tears; his cry was deep and loud, his facial expression distressed.

I stood before Adam and for one brief moment realized that I was witnessing one more stage of Adam's liberation. He could really cry now, no more crying without tears, no more screaming without sound. His physical being, his structure, was finally allowing him to express his terror, his sadness, his loneliness.

After settling Adam in his bed, in his beloved, safe room, the crying continued. I must admit that I was asking many questions. Was he sick? Was he in pain but I couldn't see it? Over and over, I came to the same conclusion: We knew what it looked like when Adam was in physical pain. I recalled the time when he was in a cast because we were attempting an archaic procedure called serial casting to correct his contractures. First, Adam was shot up with botox and then, as his arms and wrists released, he was placed in casts to hold his arms in this released place. Well, everything in his structure was moving toward collapse at that time, and his contractures were an unfortunate outcome of this collapse. His body wanted to pull up and in and hold very tight; his body did not want to be held in any other way. Adam rebelled in pain and discomfort. He let us know loudly and clearly, through body language and moaning, that he was not okay. Phil ran out into the garage, came back with a saw and cut off the cast. Adam immediately expressed relief. I remember seeing him smile. We never tried that procedure again. This time, this day, Adam seemed to be expressing something purely emotional.

I called Maribeth, the shiatsu practitioner who had been treating Adam for many years. She has a deep understanding of the flow of energy in the body, coupled with a thorough knowledge of anatomy and physiology. She also has a strong, flexible body and great intuitive ability, making her a perfect match for Adam. Maribeth had decided to use all of her well-developed skills to work with us daily, helping with ABR while continuing weekly shiatsu sessions with Adam. She never questioned the basic premise of this new therapy, believing that it complemented her own work.

Maribeth arrived within an hour, met Adam's tears, and kept her hands on him over the next few hours, using emergency shiatsu and craniosacral points. Adam would calm briefly, and Maribeth would leave to take short breaks, so I would stay with Adam. Every time he saw me, the crying would begin anew. He wanted me close; he needed to cry. Sometimes when he caught my eye, he would begin with a laugh but within seconds, his tears would return. I cried with him when I could not hold back my own release.

At one point, Maribeth was cradling Adam's head and visualized some images that she later shared with me. She had an uncanny ability to tune in to my nonverbal son's consciousness. She said three images appeared:

Adam jumping off a ski slope, his arms behind him, no snow or ground beneath him.

Adam in a hang glider, flying straight ahead, nothing in sight.

Adam in a crew boat, with people in front of him and behind, pushing him through the water.

I realized that Adam was having an intense and profound experience that day. To me, those images merely reflected how much he needed to be home, to be held, to be grounded by those who loved him.

In the early evening, Adam seemed completely spent. We gave him a Chinese herbal sleep formula, and he drifted off into a deep, restful sleep, barely moving all night. The following morning, he awakened with a smile. To be honest, I was relieved. We had given him what he needed.

In the following days, I e-mailed Leonid and talked with all of Adam's other therapists. I wanted to understand what had happened. Would it change Adam? Would this keep happening? Was there a better way to handle it? Leonid responded that it was good, an emotional catharsis. I wondered what had provoked this reaction. ABR? Acupuncture? Shiatsu? Integrated awareness? In the end, it didn't matter. Adam had been able to cry out loud and to shed wet tears. Something huge had released within his body and mind.

LOVE IS WHAT YOU ARE
ALREADY

I wasn't expecting anything. The mailman rang the doorbell and handed me a box with a postmark from Hawaii. I
immediately felt joy—any connection with my dear friends Terri
and Jenny is always gratefully welcome. It can come in the form
of an e-mail, a handmade card, a calendar, and, once, even tropical flowers from Hawaii. I will always remember those beautiful slender yellow-orange petals of the birds of paradise with the
purple interior surprise. They graced our home for weeks.

I tore open the box; as soon as I lifted the protective foam
and plastic covering, I recognized the content. Terri was craft-
ing boxes as an art form using a collage format. She had e-
mailed pictures of some of her creations, and she was thoroughly
enjoying the process. I visualized her lovingly and thoughtfully
gathering her tools—recycled tissue, greeting cards, postcards,
pamphlets, tree bark, colored paper, textured and smooth material, and paste. She was creating "forever" boxes; each was a collection of inspirational words, pictures, images, colors, and
textures. I had no idea that I was to be the recipient of one, nor
was there, in my mind, an occasion for celebration.

I carefully removed the gifted box and tenderly perused its
surfaces. My attention was immediately drawn to the words on the
very top of the box, "Love is what you are already." I recognized

the words of Byron Katie. She believes, in a wonderfully simplistic way, that our natural state is joy, peace and love so
embrace it. We all deserve no less. These words offered comfort
and I felt blessed to be reminded that I deserved freedom from
my tangled delusions.

As I held these words in my heart I gently glided my fingers over the surfaces on the box - textures of rough paper, soft
shiny golden material, crinkly tissue, smooth paper, bumpy tree
bark. The colors all melded together—green, gold, black, yellow, white, and small, narrow strips of red.

I turned the box over to examine the bottom and found a
postcard with the Chinese calligraphy for love and the explanation that this comes from the ancient pictogram showing love as
the "breath of the heart." That took my breath away.

The box appeared to be glued shut. At no point was I
tempted to force it open, not wanting to disturb any of the carefully crafted material. My thoughts were that the box was complete and I was merely to enjoy its perimeter.

A card was slipped into the mailing box with a simple message. Terri offered this gift to me to celebrate my transformation. She had walked with me for eight long years, witnessing
my pain and my joy, my fear and my courage, always there to
guide me and, sometimes, to gently prod me on my way.

I e-mailed Terri, thanking her profusely for the gift and
assuring her that I would find a place of honor for this forever
box. She made one request: I was to show it to a mutual friend
whom I would see in a few weeks.

A few weeks later, I arrived at Ange's house with my gift in
hand. She immediately took it, looked it over with deep admiration, and then started to pry it open. I said, "I think that it is
glued shut. I really don't think that we are supposed to force it
open." Ange assured me that these boxes were indeed meant to
be opened, so I stood by and watched her. The box opened to
an exquisite interior. I could not stop laughing. Each surface
was again covered with interesting images, textures, and colors.

Then I held my breath. On the bottom was a beautiful angel blowing a horn attached to the words "Love is what you are already." Given my affinity for angelic companions, this depiction was wonderfully significant.

The metaphor reverberated through me. If one is willing to risk, to move beyond the surface, sometimes with prying and tugging motions, one can reap immense reward. Transformation brings us to the interior, to the deep, inner truth about life and purpose. And this truth is exquisitely beautiful and simple.

WRITE ABOUT ME

"Write about me today," my husband said as he left with Adam on their way to school—an invitation, an opportunity. . . how could I not respond to my dear Philip?

I may as well start at the beginning. I think that he was asking me to be his mirror. He understands, this husband of mine, that I can only see him through the eyes of my deep and profound love. There will be no impartiality here.

I met Phil in Boston when I was teaching high school English and he was the vice principal (and later, principal) and, oh yes, newly sprung from an eight-year commitment to a religious order, long black robes and all. I was immediately attracted to him. Unfortunately, I was also entrenched in an intense and failing marriage. We became friends, and though I attempted many times to convince myself that we were respecting clear boundaries, something otherworldly was moving us closer and closer. In hindsight, this powerful magnetism makes perfect sense; I now know we had work to do together in this lifetime.

My marriage dissolved, and my relationship with Philip intensified. We were passionately in love, though it was hardly smooth sailing. I ran away many times, steeped in ambivalence about walking away from a marriage and needing to heal from a wounded childhood. Phil loved me and he waited.

I have always been drawn to Phil's quiet, his patience, his intelligence, and his immense loyalty. I hold loving images from our years together.

I can still see him with Aimee, our first born, sleeping on his chest as he lay sprawled on the couch.

I remember the surprise and awkwardness Phil experienced when he realized that our second-born child was a son. He had convinced himself that we would have another daughter. He was not sure that he could handle a son.

When Adam was three years old, he was hospitalized with a virulent and complex virus. It was an extremely frightening time; Adam had a high fever, blisters, insane itching, and no diagnosis. Phil climbed into the hospital bed with him to hold him, and somehow, the IV disconnected and covered them both in blood. The sight of blood made Phil nauseous.

Never interested in sports, either as a spectator or athlete, Phil embraced Adam's hockey and baseball, supporting his son through each saved goal as Adam stood in front of the net, covered in goalie gear, and through each caught ball when Adam fielded first base.

And then, of course, the turning point in our life, the hours and days after Adam's accident. Phil cried uncontrollably. He would look at me with complete dismay and say, "I can't stop." He grieved deeply, lost in despair.

I would hold him and say, "Adam will be okay." And Adam came off the ventilator and began his slow journey back.

Then Phil shook off his grief and moved into warrior mode. What a magnificent warrior he has been. His simple words to those who were responsible for our son's accident were "Tell us the truth of what happened. Accept responsibility. Apologize. Help." This was his quest, and it was unbelievably difficult and complicated—a relentless uphill battle. Phil worked a full-time job as a high school principal, helped care for both of our children, and used every spare second to research and challenge individuals, the college, and, ultimately, the State of Massachusetts for their inhumane treatment of our family. Even when the state finally relented and offered something fair to our family, Phil refused to relinquish the battle until an apology was offered. The legal settlement satisfied only one part of his hunger for justice; the lack of apology gnawed at his spirit. Friends who loved him would ask, "Do you want to be free or do you want to be right?" and he would say, "I want both."

I admired his tenacity. He demonstrates the most intensely beautiful unconditional love for our family. I long for the day when he can rest and allow his spirit to soften and lighten. I will watch him create a garden, grow vegetables, build a fish pond, and walk by the ocean.

STILL BELIEVING

One day, at exactly 11:30 a.m., a well-dressed older woman rang our doorbell and lugged her equipment into our home. She had left her home in Virginia in the early morning. She was a saleswoman, an ex-nurse, who traveled across the country selling an eye-gaze communication system.

Phil and I kept telling ourselves, in the days leading up to this visit, that we had no expectations. If it worked, wonderful; if it did not, we would continue Adam's present therapies and wait. These words are so easy to say. Feeling them, accepting them, honoring them, is not so easy.

Adam was in his bedroom just finishing a quick lunch. "Am I ready? Is he ready?" I kept trying to reign in my anxiety. "Get a grip! Just walk through the process!"

The woman, very amicable, efficiently set up the system, having needed to dismantle it for the air flight. This gave me a few moments to breathe and then time to position Adam comfortably in his wheelchair. I wheeled him into the living room, placing him directly in front of the computer screen.

"Oh God, I can't do this! I want this so badly for my son. I want this to work!" With the exception of eye blinks to simple questions, body language that we read, and sessions with our loving clairvoyant, Adam had not been able to actively participate in any other form of communication for eight years. He seemed to experience life in a passive way—the people we bring to him, the places we take him, the experiences we offer him. I had been praying earnestly for Adam to move beyond his passive positioning. Would it happen now?

The saleswoman began to tell us stories, amazing, beautiful stories about people who could finally communicate—such personal empowerment. I sat there, nodding politely. "Yes, I want that for my son too."

I was immediately not very impressed with the software for this system. She started with a dot on the screen, attempting to calibrate Adam's eye gaze and test his visual pursuit. Could his eyes track and team? I knew they could, because we had recently visited Adam's behavioral optometrist. His optometrist had been very impressed with the improvement in his visual functioning and had actually recommended this evaluation. On this visit, however, Adam, sat in his chair, not responsive to the dot. I thought, *With all of the bells and whistles of modern technology...* (my mind raced to the images of the most advanced video game graphics and the incredible animation of recently viewed movies) *...and you give him a tiny dot to track?*

I could just imagine what was going on in Adam's mind. He intensely focused on the screen, definitely trying to figure out what he was supposed to be seeing, or perhaps simply asking himself, *When does the movie come on?*

Phil could not sit silently. He stood up, walked out of the room, and returned with a small picture of a beautiful woman. He placed it over the dot, and Adam performed admirably. He followed her all over the screen and may have been thinking that he would follow her to the ends of the earth. This moment provided some comic relief, obviously, and we both calmed down a bit. At this point we were halfway there—the cup was half full.

Then we moved into new territory—volitional control. My heart beat rapidly, my throat was ready to close. Within seconds, I knew that Adam was not ready. I moved away from Adam, away from the system, away from the saleswoman, and slumped into the chair. I looked at my husband and slowly, sadly, shook my head. Phil was still watching, waiting, and exploring the possibility of getting the system and training Adam.

I watched Adam. He was frustrated and tired. The saleswoman had a stick figure cat on one side of the screen and three words on the other: "fat cat sat." Adam was being asked to move from the picture to the words on command. He may have been thinking about how boring and childish the picture and words were, or he simply may not have been able to do the task. Phil finally nodded to me. He understood; Adam was not ready.

Taking Adam's face, I tenderly applauded his hard work. I was very proud of him. We stopped, and I pushed him back into his room so he could rest and watch a movie.

I just wanted this woman to leave but she stayed for another hour, asking many questions about Adam's therapy. In her work, she sees many brain-injured clients, and Adam was an anomaly—no feeding tube, perfect eye tracking and teaming, few contractures, and so happy. She was impressed. Unfortunately, my heart was not in the conversation. I wanted this system to work, but we were only halfway there—the cup was half empty.

We said our farewell, and then Phil looked at me and said, "I'm not going to be upset. We learned something, and we will just keep going. It's okay. . . but I think we need some comfort food."

And the next morning, we still believed.

THE TANGLED WEB WE WEAVE

I lay on the acupuncturist's table and patiently waited for him to enter the room. The setting was sublime—comfortable, warm, simply decorated, and with beautiful natural and crafted lighting. My eyes welled with tears. I had been waiting for this moment; I would share a few things, and then he would offer his skillful help. He is a man who deeply understands human trauma. Through acupuncture and his spiritual perspective, I knew, he could guide me through this latest crisis. He quietly entered the room and gently coaxed the words from my mouth. I offered a strangled version of my dilemma, my tears and sobs threatening to close my throat and spill over my eyelids.

I was stuck between anger and sadness, all connected to eight years of expectation, disappointment, confusion, and frustration with my siblings. Each holiday, year after year, had heightened the intensity of their absence, both physically and emotionally. We were six adults who could not seem to find our way back to each other. There was no script to follow. My daughter, home for the holidays, had mentioned quite casually, "Mom, you are so bitter about many things." Her comment startled me. I recognized many other emotions attached to disappointment and expectation, but I never wanted to live my life from a place of bitterness. Most fortuitously, I was working with a wonderful therapist who kindly guided me to a new understanding of my family experience, holding me in a safe space while I felt the brunt of the emotions emanating from this kind of work.

I held on to a fantasy tenaciously for eight long years. I was the oldest daughter of seven children—three boys and four girls. Our parents had died, and we, by virtue of this circumstance, were responsible for one another. The fact that we had scattered all over the United States, married, and had children and careers would never interfere with this directive. FAMILY TAKES CARE OF FAMILY. I heard these words directly from my beloved mother's lips. Had she been dying of lung cancer when she had gained this perspective? Had she been feeling afraid, isolated, and in desperate need of care?

What did I want from my brothers and sisters? I wanted them to take care of me when I needed that so desperately after my son's accident. I wanted them to protect me, defend me and demonstrate unwavering loyalty. I wanted someone, anyone in my family to learn about taking care of Adam so that they could help me in a very tangible way. I wanted my family to embrace each new change and celebrate with me, encouraging me to keep going. I wanted to feel the love of my brothers and sisters. I was convinced that nothing could replace that in my heart.

By year eight, I was weary. I longed for their presence in my life, but I barely felt it—a visit here, a phone call there. I was tired of wading though the holidays in a puddle of tears. The cultural myths about family expectations during the holiday seasons only exacerbated the loss. After Adam's accident, communication between my siblings and me had broken down many times. I was in shock, traumatized, too tired to listen, and too tired to speak. I was easily offended and, evidently, according to my siblings, offensive. I do remember often painfully wondering why I could not feel their presence in my life. "Where are you? Where are you? Where are you?" Had I chased them all away? What had I done? What had I said? How could I get them to love me again? Were my actions and words truly unforgivable? Or was something else entirely different operating under the surface? My son had suffered horrifically. Was this too difficult to watch? Too difficult to get close to? Did they look at me and see a bottomless pit of need threatening to swallow them up? My brothers and sisters had each suffered their own serious losses and hardships; as a unit, could we merely not handle one more? Was the well really dry?

I finally realized that I no longer wanted to allow myself to play out the same script, to wallow in the role of either the injured party or the offender. I needed to take charge of myself, to change this very sad, depleting dynamic.

The acupuncturist nodded and felt my pulses and, with gentle compassion, said, "I can help you." After he inserted the needles, he quietly exited the room, leaving me with my silence.

The tears exploded, pouring down both sides of my face. When the needles are placed I try to remain still, not wanting to disrupt the flow of energy coursing through my body. I did not even attempt to wipe away the tears spilling onto the table. I felt a powerful release, and then I found myself visualizing the faces of my family members, each brother and each sister. Without resentment or recrimination, I said good-bye to past pain and disappointment. I released myself from the ties that bound me to that old script, and I chose my freedom from any more painful expectation.

The door opened; the needles were removed, and the acupuncturist compassionately informed me that over the next few days I would feel less heaviness. I trusted this man, and I knew that extricating myself from this dynamic of expectation would be the way to my healing.

IT WAS NOT YET TIME

I do not understand why other big events in my life did not bring me to a place of transformation—my father's death during my childhood, my mother's death before I was able to share the role of motherhood with her, and the death of my dearest brother. These losses were significant and profound, yet not life-opening for me. My son's accident, however, from the minute I engaged with the experience, brought me to the precipice. Either I related to this event on the deepest level possible or I would not survive.

I live my life differently now. I take risks and have found previously unfathomable courage. I do not live my life from a place of fear. I am not easily intimidated by other people.

Eight years had passed since Adam's near-drowning. Our legal battle of five years was long over, and one remaining obstacle continued to present itself in our life. A book was published that presented Adam's legal case, examining it from the perspective of the outdoor leadership industry. My husband had eagerly contributed one chapter to this book. The book presented several accident accounts, followed by an analysis of what went wrong and what went right. Adam's case was depicted as a bad example, a clear example of an institution failing a family. The publication of this book validated our experience, made it public, and beckoned a response from the offending institution. We waited, but nothing came. My husband challenged—no response.

We were seeking the final act—the apology, the institution expressing an apology for the unnecessary pain its process had cost this family. That was all we wanted—the public apology.

I waited; I prayed. I finally wrote my own form of a challenging e-mail to the president of the community college—one that spoke of missed opportunities, assumptions, and invitation, and one that strongly distanced us from any position of revenge or betrayal. This man was not president at the time of the accident but he had the unenviable role of handling the aftermath.

I waited again. A response to my e-mail appeared, then a phone call, and finally a scheduled visit. Perhaps an institution and its members can experience a life-opening.

Early in the morning on the day of the anticipated visit, I was deeply pensive. What help did we need? What kind of strength must we call upon?

Phil, my dearest husband, definitely needed some serenity to soothe any residual anger, frustration, or pain. He had, after all, been the warrior, waging a battle with intense tenacity and passion and had often—too many times to count—been rebuffed and stifled.

I had envisioned the goal of the meeting being reconciliation. I believed that we all needed to understand that when we are limited by sorrow, bereavement, grievances, or bitterness we are actually destroying the vitality and enjoyment of the ever-present now.

The president of the college finally sat in our living room. We looked at him, offering no bitterness, no recriminations—only a challenge: Are you ready to apologize? We are ready to listen, accept, and forgive.

I asked him why he had finally decided to respond to us. He said, "I am here because I want a new beginning." I was puzzled by this comment. Had he not just passed the FOR SALE sign at the bottom of our driveway? We were leaving, moving on. There was only one thing that would make our departure easier—the public apology. He sat with this, unable or unwilling to comment.

A memory was triggered in my consciousness. We were sitting in the same room with the chairman of the Board of Trustees of this community college. My husband and I told her what we needed, and her response was, "We can't give you what you need, but perhaps we can give you something else." Was this theme about to be reiterated?

The president said, "Why isn't it enough that I am sitting here in your living room? I want to tell you that things are different now at our school. Adam's accident and your actions precipitated institutional change." The president said, "Sharon, I want you to know that hardly a day goes by that I don't think about your son, your Adam."

At that moment, sadly, these sentiments were not enough. The visit ended, and we were left in that frustrating space of the unresolved. It was unacceptable. Obviously, the time for apology had not yet arrived. We had to wait. Leaving this community without the apology felt unbearable.

THE SADNESS BENEATH THE CELEBRATION

Adam coughed, his consistent signal for "I'm awake. Come to me." I entered his room singing "Happy Birthday." He lay in his bed with a sleepy smile. Later, I would read his cards to him and unwrap his presents. Most likely, he would receive sports memorabilia on this birthday. He was such a devoted spectator. I presented him with his birthday balloon— a beautiful butterfly this year. *Will this be the year you come out of your cocoon, dear son?* Other years, his room had been filled with frogs and fish and multi-colored balloons. His beautiful eyes glistened with excitement, anticipation, and joy. He knew that today was special, and he had been promised an outing and a luscious dessert.

After I washed his handsome face and brushed his teeth, I dressed him in an outfit I had specifically selected for this day. He would be wearing a Boston Bruins sweatshirt and matching sweatpants given to him by his sister, Aimee. I slid his contracted feet into warm slippers; his shoes had become too uncomfortable. After I fed him some breakfast, I gently eased him out of his bed. As I placed him in front of his wheelchair, he giggled as we stood nose to nose. I embraced him lovingly, silently acknowledging the incredible miracle of his existence. I stood holding him, kissing him and caressing his hair. I was not mournfully clutching a 12-year-old's photo at some forlorn cemetery, hovering by his gravestone embellished with beautiful thoughts about the hereafter. I was celebrating 21 years of his life today. I was grateful, and I was sad.

I pushed his wheelchair down the ramp through the garage and out into the cold and misty rain. It was a short distance to the van. I maneuvered his chair into the van and securely locked it into place. I turned on his DVD player and placed his wireless earphones on his head, shifting his head just so, directing his gaze to the screen.

We arrived at the movie theater; the line for tickets was ominously long, and I made a quick decision. I placed myself directly at the front of the line and politely requested that I be allowed to cut in because waiting would be too difficult for my son. The line opened, and people stepped back, not at all surprised or offended by my request.

We entered the small theater and sat in the designated wheelchair section. Unfortunately, it's an open aisle, so people walked in front of Adam in a stream. He followed people with his gaze, his phenomenal visual pursuit, which removed his gaze from the screen. I had to get up out of my seat each time and gently direct him back to the screen. I also had to protect his slipper-covered feet because unaware people bang into the wheelchair and hit his feet.

We had given Adam five milligrams of Valium to cope with this extremely stimulating environment. He was calm and collected. Phil and I, on the other hand, were ready to jump out of our seats to scream, "Please, use another aisle to get to your seat! Can't you see that you are walking right in front of us?" *We* needed the Valium.

The lights dimmed, the audience quieted, the previews passed, and we settled in to watch the movie. Adam was obviously engaged and enjoying himself, smiling and laughing at the physical comedy. People continued to walk in front of us during the movie, but Adam, thankfully, was oblivious. He was connected and happy. I was grateful and I was sad.

At the movie's end, we quickly pushed Adam out of the theater to avoid the crowding at the exit. Now it was time for the second part of his birthday adventure—the hot fudge sundae. His eyes twinkled when I placed it before him. I spooned each mouthful—a little ice cream, a bit of hot fudge, and a dollop of whipped cream—into his mouth. He moved the ice cream around with his tongue, swallowed, and opened his mouth for the next spoonful. He devoured an entire sundae.

We then walked through a store and bought a New England Patriots winter cap and a Red Sox bolster. We had completed our adventure, and we departed for home. When I entered the house, I realized that I did not want to put Adam into bed yet. I needed to hold him. I did not know whether he needed that from me, but I humored myself. I helped him out of the chair and set him on a low stool. I then sat behind him and held him close. My son, a young adult, had celebrated his 21st birthday. I was grateful and I was sad.

THE POWER OF CEREMONY

My son's accident presented the greatest personal growth opportunity of my life. It didn't happen in a vacuum, though— I recognized the intense need for direction and guidance, having never before traversed the twists and turns so plentiful on our particular human journey.

This was the ninth anniversary. I walked into this day absolutely refreshed, having spent three days in Florida with my daughter walking the beach, collecting shells, reading a book, taking naps, and swimming. I felt guilty for exactly one hour about leaving my husband and son. The days were filled with blissful nothingness, so on this ninth year of July 24ths, I was experiencing ease, deep cleansing breathing, and clarity—something I had not known for many years...maybe not ever.

Terri was visiting from Hawaii and had offered to come to our home to perform a ceremony to commemorate this day. Ange, my therapist and good friend to Terri, wanted to accompany her. Phil, Adam, and I had always spent this anniversary alone, many years entrenched in guilt, disappointment, and isolation, though the healing power of time had begun to minimize the sting of the day.

Terri had been teaching me that spiritual ceremonies help us create safe places for our most complicated feelings so we don't have to haul them around with us forever. On this day, I believed that we needed to clear out some residue. Phil and I had been looking at our life and measuring with unusual clarity what was adding and what was taking away from our life's quality. We had not managed to sell our house after a year and a half of open houses and private showings—too many to count. We also felt enmeshed in some relationships with people that continually led to hurt, disappointment, frustration, and anger. We were stuck.

I welcomed Terri and Ange into our home, and we talked briefly about what we thought we needed. Out of the blue, my dear husband said, "Oh, besides the house and all of the emotional stuff with family and friends, can you work on Sharon's level of trust with people in relation to Adam?" I was not prepared for that one—and I felt targeted. Terri was watching me. She immediately knew what work had to be done in this moment and on this day. My face was burning, and Terri lovingly described what she had just witnessed. She had watched my heart close down when my husband suggested that I had an issue with trust and Adam. She directed Ange and me to accompany her to an upstairs bedroom, just the three of us.

I looked back at Adam and Phil as I slowly climbed the stairs, envying their non-participation. I was thinking, *Here we go again. At least I'm not driving in a blizzard to find my father's gravesite this time. What could be more difficult than that?*

We entered a bare bedroom (cleared because of our anticipated move), and Ange spread out candles, flowers, water, and honey. Then she placed some incense and rosemary in an ashtray to burn. I was told to lie flat on the floor, eyes closed. The intent of the ceremony was to put prayer and light into our desire to change, to become "unstuck."

Terri anointed my face, my ears, my eyes, the palms of my hands, and the bottoms of my feet with water. She sang while she moved around my body, a prayerful song about a bird from the Amazon jungle called Kanaro. I remember her saying, "Just receive the words. It's not important that you know the story."

The incense burned, and I breathed in the smoke. Then I felt and tasted honey on my lips. Ange was holding my head throughout the anointing. Finally, Terri placed her hand over my heart and uttered the words, "You are reborn, Sharon." At that exact moment, the ashtray with the burning incense exploded, and shards of glass went flying everywhere.

I was startled, but I had learned to always expect the unexpected in my new life, and especially when I am near my beloved friend and guide, Terri. Without missing a beat, Ange and Terri quickly gathered the burning residue, helped me up off the floor, and guided me down the stairs and out the door. I felt like I was in a trance and was thinking, *Okay, I have been reborn. What else needs to be done?*

Ange and Terri had much more in mind for me. We began by walking the perimeter of the house four times, and then Ange suggested that we needed to stop and provide an opportunity to release some very complicated feelings from my newly opened heart. According to these two amazingly intuitive women, there was no better time. Ange looked at our backyard, our freshly grown grass above our brand new septic system, and motioned, saying, "This is perfect."

And there, on that spot right above the septic system, with love, support, and guidance, I unleashed my hurt, disappointment, frustration, anger, and bitterness. I was held by Terri and motivated and coached by Ange. Ange is a beautiful woman who has passionately embraced her rich Italian heritage. She believes in the power of expressing anger through strong, bold, guttural language. I heard Terri whispering, "First comes the anger, then the sadness." I turned my head and saw Ange kneeling in anticipation of pounding the earth with her fists to support my anger.

"Sharon, use your voice! Who are you angry with?"

The words were sticking to my tongue with relentless tenacity, so Ange began for me. "Damn your father!" I remembered the father who had deserted me when I was eight years old when he left this life on a lonely dark road.

"Damn your grandfather!" I remembered the grandfather whose predatory hands had robbed me of my childhood innocence.

Deep, deep wounds. I opened my mouth. Yes, I was trying. . . .It was so hard, too hard. Ange continued the rant. She named my pain, and her voice became my voice.

We stopped, and then I convulsed in sobs. I heard Terri. "Yes, you have been so alone, alone for so long." My body heaved, and I felt Terri's arms around me. When I tired, she continued with those tears of intense sadness. Her tears became my tears.

Eventually—maybe it was minutes or maybe an hour, I don't know—I rolled over and sat up. Ange stood up and ran into the house. She returned with a bowl of ripe, succulent blueberries. She said, "And now you will receive, just receive." I sat there, cross-legged in the rich grass above the septic tank, my eyes closed, being fed one berry after another until every berry had been received.

We rejoined Adam and Phil in our living room, and then I read a petition I had written calling upon divine intervention in the sale of our house. I also added a request for help in trusting that new people would enter our life with the distinct intention of joining our journey with Adam.

With intense gratitude, I said good-bye to Terri and Ange. Then I became silent. I had to have some space to integrate every word and every action of the past few hours. Fortunately, Phil and I have that perfect distance—he would not intrude. We did have one more thing to do on this day, and it felt critical. We drove to Charlemont, to the site of the accident. I brought the leftover gifts from the ceremony—the honey, the water, and the ashes from the burned incense. Phil stayed with Adam as I made my way down to the river, walking the same path I had used many times. This time, the path was overgrown.

I could barely find my footing, and I was unable to navigate my way to the edge to be close to the rock that had entrapped my beautiful son. I could not recognize anything. A group of rafters floated by, laughing and spinning their way through the moving waters. I just stopped, found a way to the river's edge, and knelt down to offer my gifts to the river.

It was cloudy, and I felt the shadows of the trees holding me. I stood in silent prayer for a long while. About a quarter of a mile up the river, I could see sunlight breaking through the clouds, so I waited. I waited until it reached me; draped in light, I clearly spoke. "Good-bye, river. I won't be back. We have had a long relationship, you and I. At first I was deeply terrified, actually, horror-stricken in your presence, and now I can stand here and pray with you and feel your sacredness." With tears of joy mixed with some sadness, I slowly climbed away from the river.

We headed home along the twisty, narrow roads of the Mohawk Trail. I was still unable to speak to Phil. As we came down Green Mountain a short distance from our home, my cell phone rang. "You have an offer on your home."

The following morning, I was standing in Adam's bedroom, which was located directly in front of the septic system. Through the window, in the exact spot where I had lain, I saw a thick, long branch standing tall and straight, nestled deep into the earth. It was not a dream.

THE UNANTICIPATED

I recognized the return address. I couldn't rip open the envelope fast enough. The words on the card blurred: "Colleen died in Arizona yesterday. After a long and courageous battle with cancer she requested to come off life support and was gone within twenty minutes. The ripples of the victims of this story continue to manifest themselves."

The card had been sent by an ex-administrator of the community college to spare us the shock of reading this news in our daily paper.

Colleen had been a key player in the drama that had significantly and unalterably changed my family's life. She was the counselor who had made the decision to supervise 12 young boys split into two separate groups, one group with her, one group farther downstream, while they practiced a victim-rescue maneuver at the Deerfield River on July 24, 1998. She had given the signal for my son to jump into the moving waters and then, for one split second, turned to answer a question. She had looked back, and then Adam was underwater. Her attempt to save him by swimming to him had failed; the current was too fast, and his foot had been entrapped. Colleen had screamed for help, sent some of the boys up the riverbank, and then watched as rafters, guides, and then emergency personnel had taken over.

I dropped the card and slowly moved over to the couch until I could feel the cushions behind my knees. I allowed my body to collapse. I was stunned and sad and, at that moment, oblivious to the myriad emotions that would surface over the next few days and weeks.

The first time my husband and I had seen this young woman was about six weeks after the accident, at the Connecticut Rehabilitation Hospital. I remembered a young Colleen, probably in her early 20's. She and the other counselor, who had left the river site early to drive a boy and his friend to meet his parents, thereby leaving her alone, had requested that they be allowed to visit Adam. Adam had been stabilized then, off the ventilator, but certainly not the young boy they had supervised during the week long summer camp. My husband and I had both been present during their visit. When these two young people stood by Adam's bed all we had witnessed was their youth and their pain. We had offered our forgiveness.

Once Adam was home, Colleen had called and asked to visit a few times, and she remembered his birthday for a couple of years. The next time we saw her was at our invitation. She attended our ceremony at the Deerfield River to celebrate Adam's life. I remember her mother hovering protectively by her side. At some point, and this is foggy for me, either before the ceremony or shortly after, we heard that she had been diagnosed with cancer.

We heard nothing more from her until her deposition. We knew that she was very sick, out of the country, and potentially would be videotaping the interview. However, at the last minute, Colleen returned to Massachusetts. We made the decision to bring Adam with us and we drove to a local bank where the deposition was scheduled to take place. Never, ever had we questioned her about that day and she had never offered her story. I remember feeling that I finally would have the rich opportunity to hear the full story from her perspective. We met in a cold, corporate conference room. I was shocked by

Colleen's appearance. The young slender, athletic woman of 1998 was gone. She was puffy and walked tentatively on the arm of her mother. I sat there and looked from this very sick young woman to Adam—such a profound impact. I remember her well-rehearsed answers. "Stick to the questions, don't offer anything else," and show little to no emotion.

I waited for days after receiving the short message in the mail. I wanted to read her obituary in our local newspaper. She had died in the Southwest, so there was a long lapse as preparations were made for her local funeral. I searched for a condolence card, pictured myself at the wake. We are all one; we have all suffered; we are all victims. There was an inexplicable connection.

When I eventually had the obituary in my hands, I found myself in an unexpected place. Phrases caught my eye: "despite the many obstacles placed in her path, she lived each day to its fullest, making friends wherever she went" and "She was well-known by many as a beloved swimming instructor." I snapped. I was angry, full of a dark all-consuming rage. I was wading through a bubbling cesspool. I had never allowed myself to feel angry with this young woman. I had made excuses: She was only 21, so young, harmless, and inexperienced at life. I had forgiven her for her decisions on that fateful day at the river. I recalled that day at the hospital when I offered my forgiveness, only to remember with remarkable vividness that it had not been requested.

Then the questions inside my heart screamed out, "Colleen, how could you have placed my son in such an unsafe environment? Colleen, did you ever think about Adam as you traveled through your life? Colleen, was Adam one obstacle placed on your path, something to overcome and leave behind?"

I could only hold these questions momentarily. I was so uncomfortable with this rage. It provoked shame, guilt, and embarrassment. Colleen suffered, and she died. Leave it alone. And then I turned on myself—how could I feel this way? I honestly did not know how to get beyond this so that, at the very least, I could look at myself in the mirror and not feel horrified. I wrote for five days—a beginning, a middle, and an end. Yes, I needed to get to the end.

The first day, I ranted. The second day, I visualized Colleen sitting in a chair directly in front of me. I pleaded for help as I tried to bring this rage to an end and to allow her peace. And the questions poured out: Did you like my son? Did you shed tears on that day and in the days, weeks, months and years that followed? For Adam? For his family? For yourself? Did we frighten you when we filed a lawsuit? Did you pray for Adam? Did you hold Adam responsible for his behavior on that day? Did you hold yourself responsible?

I framed each question tentatively, again battling the guilt behind each thought. The answers did not seem important; the mere opportunity to ask the questions was what my heart and mind longed for. In the best of all worlds, would it not have been wonderful for all of the parties impacted by this event to have been given the time and space to actually formulate their most important questions and thoughts and offer them to each other? We are all one; we have all suffered. Not in this world, not in this litigious culture, not in this lifetime, not soon enough for this young woman and this family. A very painful example of missed opportunity.

By the fourth and fifth days, I accepted that I knew very little about how my son's accident had impacted this woman's life and, honestly, it was not my business. I will never know if that day changed Colleen. I am only responsible for releasing these painful thoughts from my own consciousness. Dwelling in the territory of unasked, unanswered questions kept me in the role of victim. Not today and not tomorrow.

VISITING ADAM

David wanted to visit. David is a handsome young man attending Babson College and majoring in entrepreneurship. He excelled in basketball and golf in our local high school, and he was Adam's best friend.

Adam and David climbed trees, built forts, rode bikes, exuding wonderful, typical boy energy. My husband and I would take them out on the river in our motorboat and pull over to the river's edge, and they would climb out and swim beneath the overhanging branches, imagining they were pirates and explorers. They outgrew these games and moved on to exploring our property, driving in a beaten-up old golf cart, traversing the bumps and hills with recklessness. David always made me swear to never tell his mother.

The boys went to different schools in the sixth grade, and some distance was created in their friendship. Adam had his first girlfriend and was learning how to dance and to dress stylishly. He talked on the phone for hours and played love songs. David focused on his new school and played basketball. Adam played hockey.

The summer of the accident, they played baseball together. And then, of course, their friendship changed dramatically when Adam could not ride a bike, climb a tree, talk on the phone, throw a baseball or sing a love song. None of these seemed to matter to David, though. He wanted that friendship to continue.

Initially, Adam's friends came in groups and with their parents. David's mother came with him for the first few visits. Then David came alone. His mother or father would drop him off at the end of the driveway, and he would walk up the steep hill, knock on the door, and come in to sit with Adam. He visited every few months and then less frequently. During high school, his visiting ceased. When this happened, I understood. David was the only friend who had maintained any contact with Adam. He was a teenager with a very full life. I just assumed that he, like so many others, was just getting on with his life and that he had forgotten Adam.

To visit or not to visit; it's complicated and intense for all involved. The visits are awkward and uncomfortable. In the beginning, shortly after the accident, when people entered our home and had to come face-to-face with the transformation of a normal, healthy, vibrant, athletic 12-year-old into a rigid, nonverbal, nonreactive suffering, contracted boy, it was horrific, especially for Adam's friends.

Whose job was it to make people feel more comfortable? Whose responsibility was it to give them hope? Whose task was it to explain brain injury? Who needed to be the teacher, counselor, and caretaker? Should I, as mother, have shouldered this burden? How does one make a situation like this more palatable? I wondered, *If people are too uncomfortable, they will never come again. Will that be my fault?*

Our community was so good in the initial stages of the crisis; however, there doesn't seem to be a script for the long term. We all faced a heart-wrenching dilemma. Adam was not able to return to his life, school, friends, and sports. Over time, people disengaged, unplugged. It was too hard to watch. The culture of our community affirmed this position: If something is too hard, then walk away.

David went away to college, and during his first break, he called to arrange a visit with Adam. I am ashamed to admit this, but I found myself cowering in discomfort. David called several times before I answered the phone. What would he expect to see . . . Adam walking and talking? So much of Adam's healing is not visible to the eye.

I had been told that David had written about Adam for a college essay. Obviously, he had continued to hold Adam close to his heart. I could not deny his visit. When David arrived, I saw that his transformation was dramatic. He had grown into a tall, handsome, muscular young man. He was also very kind. He greeted Adam warmly, touched his hand, and stood directly in front of his eyes. Adam was delighted. Then David sat down by Adam's side while Adam had therapy, and we chatted.

I thought the visit went extremely well; however, I was exhausted. I had worked so hard to make everyone comfortable. I wanted David to be hopeful and educated about recovery from brain injury. I wanted him to have a good experience, to believe that Adam was healing and, most importantly, to return.

David returned for another visit. This time, my goal was to honor both of these young men, David and Adam. I wanted to welcome David into my home, accept that he cared for my son, and just allow them to be together, to enjoy each other's company. I would not interfere or impose my need to make everyone comfortable and educated. I intended to relax, breathe, and enjoy watching these two old friends spend some time together.

The joy in both young men's faces was incredible. Adam laughed, and David smiled warmly. He took his seat at Adam's feet at the end of Adam's therapy table, and while Adam received his therapy over two hours, David held his feet and Adam watched David's face while we chatted. Adam was so intensely watching and listening that he exhausted himself. He could not keep his eyes open and drifted off to sleep. Only then would David get up and excuse himself. Now that I had removed myself from the role of everyone's caretaker, I was able to see David's genuine interest and warmth. He truly cared about Adam and wanted to spend time with him under any conditions.

The next day, I called David's mother. I needed to tell her that her son was a magnificent human being and I was clearly aware that his parents had something to do with this. She accepted this praise with gratitude and then helped me to understand that the visits were very important to David. He kept a picture of Adam on the front visor of his car. He looked forward to these visits and always returned to his family full of hope and stories. To him, Adam always looked better.

A DAY IN THE LIFE

A mother mindfully watches over her child. I did that in a normal way for Adam's first 12 years. After his accident, I watched him in a very different way. I learned to read my silent boy's body language, a skill I honed over the years through my hyper-vigilance. Sometimes—actually, many times—I wondered how he might be experiencing his world, and I imagined his thoughts as he entered one of his days. Who knows a son better than his mother?

Ugh. . . not yet, I'm still tired. The purring machine is to my right. I can feel the ever so slight pulsations from the inflating/deflating air bladders placed on both sides of my pelvis. I fall asleep each night to this sound and vibration and I awaken each morning to the same. It's not bad. I can't roll around, so it's not cramping my sleep style. I do feel my body beginning to unwind, and I can hear my mother saying, "From the inside out and from top to bottom." So many years now, so tight, and now the softening, the letting go... It feels good.

Now my mother quietly unhooks the machine and moves me ever so gently onto my side. The shades are still drawn, the room dark. It feels good to turn over, off my back. Mom then places a roll of foam and an air bladder on my back, restarts the machine, and tiptoes out of my room. Ah, back to sleep—closing eyes, drifting, dreaming. I know that I have at least another hour of rest.

The door opens. Light, music, shades drawn, machine unhooked. What will Mom choose this morning? Mozart, Tibetan metal bowls, chanting? I never know what to expect. I have to wake up—no arguing. My mother has me on a strict schedule. It's okay. I understand that I am quite the work in progress and it means labor-intensive days—two to five hours of manual therapy and usually 14 hours of machine. I know that every effort is made to entertain me during these therapy marathons, and I appreciate that. I watch old and new movies, sports, situation comedies, and even **Ellen**. *I laugh when she dances. Most of the time, I do not complain. However, there are those moments. How would you like someone covering your ear, cheek, or neck with a small foam-filled ball—sitting there for 45 minutes, pumping it? It does not hurt, honestly. It's a very gentle compression. I just feel annoyed sometimes. And maybe I complain because I want you to know that I have a voice.*

My mother stands at the side of my bed, waiting. I can feel her presence. She wants me to open my eyes and turn toward her. She is very persistent; actually, downright annoying. I open my eyes, and I even smile. This seems to make her happy.

She washes my face. I wonder if she knows that the crap she puts on my face after she washes it stings. She lets it dry and then shaves me, feeds me my boring pureed breakfast. It all tastes the same to me, no matter what she does to it. She brushes my teeth—I do hate the flossing part—combs my hair, and dresses me… comfortable soft clothes, please. Ugh, not today, I guess. Instead, she struggles to put a nice shirt and jeans on me. Uh-oh—must be going somewhere today.

Hey, where's my dad? He usually makes an appearance by now. He makes me laugh every time I see him. I don't know anyone who can act as goofy as him yet still be the strongest man I'll ever know. Yeah, Dad is my hero. I trained him well. Hah! Dad is cleaning up. Mom says we both need to be presentable.

Meeting new people is not easy for me. Sometimes it's boring because people forget to talk to me. I sit there patiently waiting for someone to strike up a conversation, and it does not happen very often. People will say, "Hi, Adam," but they don't understand that unless I am looking at them, eye-to-eye, I am not really connecting, and I really like to hear what people have to say. Too often, I feel invisible. Maybe things will be different this time.

APOLOGY

Apology, forgiveness, closure, peace, and joy, this was my mantra for one solid year. On my daily walks I repeated the mantra over and over again—apology, forgiveness, closure, peace, and joy. We had unfinished business with the college, the unwilling and unknowing partner to my son's karmic challenge. Begrudgingly and within the rigid boundaries delineated by our litigious culture, the community college had met its obligations. We had agreed on a settlement, something to help with Adam's long-term care. But the voices kept murmuring, "It's not enough. It's not over."

We made our decision to leave the community of Greenfield. We combed through 19 years of collected memories and belongings. The house was now uncluttered, freshly painted, repaired, and glossy clean. And then we waited. . . It was a year and a half of open houses and private showings before the right buyer arrived, freeing us to find a new home in a new community. Throughout these months, the voices never quieted—there was still work to be done with the college.

One day, I was walking an unusual route, seeking a steep incline—working my heart, I guess. I entered one of the wealthier sections in Greenfield. Trudging up the hill, I came face-to-face with the college president. I did not know that this was his neighborhood, and I was shocked to see him. Shocked may not be the right word. I harbored myriad feelings toward him—frustration and livid rage were at the top of the list, primarily because so many of our pleas and gestures for closure beyond the settlement had been repeatedly rebuffed, often wordlessly—the old nonresponse tactic. I had met him many times over the past nine years—in our home, in his office, in the Massachusetts Attorney General's office, and in a mediator's office. Our relationship with this school and the state was extremely contentious. My husband, in particular, was relentless in his passionate need to be heard; he would do anything to get to the truth, to shock the conscience of this community of educators and politicians. Phil went to the media many times; he even appeared with Adam at the college president's inaugural ceremony (as I mentioned previously, this man was not in the president's position at the time of the accident, but he inherited the case and the rancor). Phil was determined to not allow our situation to fade into the background.

On this day, on my walk, I was face to face with this man—in his neighborhood with his young daughter playing close by. I extended my hand, and he greeted me. He merely said, "You know that Phil has been trying to meet with me." I found myself nodding, and then I just started talking, no formality, no witnesses, just he and I. I told him about my husband, the man he barely knew because he had kept him at arm's length for years and years. I asked him to listen to Phil. I discreetly pointed to his daughter and acknowledged that I was grateful that he was a father. I asked him to listen to Phil with his father's heart.

Something shifted, and we began to move in a completely new direction. We entered mediation for months and months with the goal of moving beyond the settlement and into the humane business of reconciliation. We selected a mediator known to both sides, a man who seemed perfectly capable of maintaining the necessary impartiality to facilitate a highly emotional long-term struggle—the perceived needs of the institution versus the perceived needs of the family.

Phil and I were very direct. We felt that we deserved, needed, and wanted an apology, a meaningful apology, a public apology. There is nothing simple about asking an institution for this type of action. We knew this, and we expected the college president to rise above the complexity and get it done. Many changes had occurred at the college, something which could definitely work in our favor. The Board of Trustees had changed; the new chairperson was open to the process. We, the parents, had softened and healed, and our message was easier to hear.

Also, as a group—Bob, the college president, Phil and I, and David, the mediator, all believed that it was the right thing to do. And I continued my silent mantra—apology, forgiveness, closure, peace, and joy.

Sitting in mediation was intense. During every session, my admiration and respect for the college president increased. Bob remembered that we had waited nine years. He accepted that we had no reason not to be overly reactive when the lines of communication within the institution broke down. He was empathic and listened with an open heart. He only pleaded for time to get everyone in the college on board. He wanted to present a united front and support for the apology. I do remember one pivotal moment when we were impatient with the painfully long process. I was sitting across from him and he was wondering if we would find an apology meaningful if he ultimately needed to stand alone as the college president and offer it on his own. I looked at him with weeping eyes and said, "I am in awe and gratitude that you would do this for us."

He put his head down and said, "Sharon, don't thank me. Please don't thank me."

One last meeting with pivotal members of the community college was scheduled. The apology was ready, having been carefully crafted by our small group. All we needed was general approval. They would not preview the apology; they only needed to agree to the gesture. I waited by the phone, trying not to pace, staring at the phone, willing it to ring. I lost patience, grabbed the phone, and called the mediator. He said, "yes."

The actual reading of the apology was to take place the following day in front of faculty and staff, no media. Bob had a well-choreographed plan in his head for the presentation. We entered the assembly hall—Phil, Adam, and I placed directly in front of the staff. Through the reading of a profoundly moving short story, Bob adeptly coaxed the staff and readied them for the apology. People in the audience were nodding, hearts were opening.

Bob then turned to us and began to read. "All too much needless pain and suffering was added to this family's already painful journey. I understand the degree to which our behavior caused that for them. In the final analysis, Greenfield Community College had a responsibility to their family to reach out and embrace them, to say that 'together we will walk this painful and difficult path.' We failed to live up to that responsibility. We failed to reach out to them in a most basic and humane way. At times our behavior was inhumane and unresponsive. I do deeply apologize on behalf of all of Greenfield Community College."

I had no doubt in that moment, in that room, we were all involved in a huge karmic healing. People were weeping, both men and women. There was not one tiny morsel of animosity—only catharsis and healing. The assembly dispersed, and people stood in line to embrace us, to weep in our arms, and to stand before our beautiful son. Adam sat there in all of his glory, attentive and responsive, greeting their tears with his joy. And the voice said, "It's over now."

SOBERING MOMENTS

I methodically combed through the house, gathering everything we needed for this trip to Montreal—not just clothes, not just appropriate food for Adam's ever-evolving eating issues, not just Adam's favorite movies, and not just pillow props and wedges to make Adam comfortable in the hotel bed. No, we also had to bring all of the therapy tools. You see, I am the keeper, the organizer, the fluffer, the head of Team Adam. I load the towels, foam, rubber bands, melons, candies, rolls, balls, and accompanying sponges into one large plastic container. Into another tub, I place the "precious as gold" ABR machine with all of the hoses, bladders, and foam setups. These two plastic containers hold the tools my son desperately needs to improve the quality of his life.

My husband packed the van, and when Maribeth arrived, we were ready to leave, with just enough room for everyone to safely and comfortably sit. A movie was started for Adam; I sat in the front, resting. We had been making this trip now for five years, and though I am quite adept at the packing and planning, it still exhausted me.

The dance began...another five-hour trip to Montreal, checking into our hotel, unloading the van, and heading to the ABR Center for Adam's evaluation. Everything proceeded smoothly, though we waited a few hours for the evaluation. I had come to expect this, and it did not upset me. We may have to wait, but once we were in the actual evaluation, time stood still. This time was ours, and we were always granted complete attention. Leonid greeted us and began his examination. I sat there, as always, counting the number of times Leonid used the words "remarkable," "amazing," and "good." He examined every fold of skin and every body part as he methodically searched for change. We returned to the hotel tired and happy.

Days three, four, and five were packed with hours of training—new exercises, new tools, and much sought-after conversation with other parents. Supposedly, we were not allowed to chat during the trainings, but we stole moments when the trainers were busy elsewhere. We are a community of believers; we are a community of doers; we are willing to work hard, think outside of the "tried and true" and run the marathon. Leonid constantly reminds all of us that this journey is not a sprint; we must commit to this labor-intensive, slow-moving, ever-evolving, long-term approach to brain injury.

We had time over these few days to eat, sleep, take care of Adam, and navigate the crowded streets of Montreal to travel to the ABR Center. By the end, we had eight new manual and seven new machine exercises. This would hold us for the next six months. We left Montreal after five days and reached the border by early afternoon.

I took a turn driving after lunch, and my husband rested in the front passenger seat. So far, I would have described this trip as uneventful. In the past, we have had our van stolen, Adam had been sick enough one time to stop training and return home, and we had also been stopped at the border and questioned at length. Not this time—I sat comfortably in the driver's seat and breathed deeply—almost home.

Suddenly, my husband sat up straight and began fumbling through the papers on the console that separates the front seats. He demanded to know what I had done with his napkin from lunch. I told him calmly, because I was still feeling my deep breaths, that I had cleaned the litter out of the car during our last stop. He informed me, with outrage, that I had thrown away his partial denture. We were at least 25 miles from the border. I wanted to turn around, but he was insistent. "NO!" he said. "We won't be able to find them, and we will have to wait at the border again because the stop was right before we left Canada. Adam is getting tired, and we are halfway home." He sat and silently fumed. I kept sneaking glances at him. He was intractable. None of my apologies reached him. We did not speak for the rest of the trip. Maribeth, the therapist who had accompanied us, witnessed this entire drama, much to my dismay. Somewhere deep in my mind, I knew that this scene could be hilariously funny, but I could not allow myself to even consider that possibility. We spiraled downward. We rarely argue; we are a team; we have to be a team. The silence was unbearable. I could not make this right. I was exhausted and numb; my husband was exhausted and numb. So, this was where our "big life" brought us. We took on an enormous challenge; we met it daily, and now we were sitting in frozen silence over a set of dentures. I knew in my heart that something far deeper was troubling Phil, but I couldn't go there—I was too tired.

We arrived home, unpacked, and settled Adam into bed. We tried to talk, but we were unable to reach any resolution. He kept telling me that I did not understand what I had done. I tossed and turned all night, thinking, *Figure it out, figure it out.*

The next morning, I dragged myself out of bed, readied Adam for school, and fielded a weepy phone call from our daughter. She was moving and wanted our help. She also had a sick puppy. I was not able to listen or help. I went to my acupuncturist's office instead.

"Listen, my husband is falling apart in front of my eyes; my daughter can't seem to find anyone to help her besides me, and my son needs me all of the time. My chest is tight, and I have a lump in my throat."

I fell onto the heated table, and the needles took me to a quiet place. Slowly, I practiced a few breaths. My lungs began to open, and I was breathing deeper. I was on my way out.

So, the big picture—my husband felt that I had not taken care of him or watched out for him. I was able to hear him eventually. I said "no" to my daughter. She has many friends, and they helped her move and took care of her puppy. This time she was on her own. I realized that I could say "no" to her and it did not mean that I did not love her enough. Also, and most importantly, I needed to take care of myself.

TRINKETS

People often asked me to tell them about the young, pre-accident Adam. Many years passed before I was able, without the suffocating presence of grief, to hold Adam's first 12 years of life in a place of loving memory. I remember one particularly poignant night that in hindsight allows me to describe my son of yesterday and my transformed son of today.

I was trying to sleep, though it was nothing but restless tossing and turning. Adam had not yet returned from his outing. It was the early part of the summer after his sixth-grade year. I would roll over, look at the clock, and try to will myself back to sleep. Finally, nearing midnight, I heard him. Adam slammed the front door, not out of rudeness but a 12-year-old's intense excitement. He wanted us to wake up; he never did like being in the house alone. Sleeping parents gave him no comfort.

He noisily bolted into our bedroom, switched on the light, and flopped down on the side of the bed, my side. "Mom, I just had the best night of my life." On this magical night, he had attended his first Red Sox game at Fenway with his entire baseball team and coaches. He chattered on, oblivious to the hour. Then he had to show me his new stash. Whenever Adam went anywhere special, he felt compelled to buy something to remember his fun—a trinket, a thing of little value except to the heart. I often found myself refraining from uninvited comments like,

"Do you really need that?" or "That doesn't seem worth its price." On this evening, he had returned with a flashy Red Sox keychain and a framed baseball card. I don't even remember the player. He eventually relaxed enough to sleep, but only after placing his new treasures in the small wooden box by his bed, a place reserved for only the best.

Adam didn't indulge in just trinkets. When you entered his bedroom, you would immediately see collections everywhere: miniature hockey pucks, baseball and hockey trading cards, shelves filled with matchbox cars, pendants from hockey and baseball teams, and a variety of stuffed animals. Sometimes they were displayed in an orderly fashion, sometimes scattered throughout the room. On a bookcase he kept his vacation mementos: those silly little stick boats in tiny plastic bottles, a sketch of himself inside a *South Park* cartoon drawn by a local artist in Maine, boxes of seashells (he was particularly fond of sand dollars), key chains shaped like surfboards, and postcards from Maine, South Carolina, Florida, and Virginia.

I held each of these treasures months after the accident, knowing that he had selected, held, admired, and possibly loved each one, despite their miniscule monetary value. I sobbed when I eventually recognized that he could no longer walk the stairs to the second floor, that he could no longer sit on his bedroom floor and admire his collected life. I packed up his room, and it remained absolutely empty.

A new collection entered his life while he was in the Intensive Care Unit. Adam was hooked up to a ventilator, and his friends needed to see him. A social worker had taken a picture of him in his new precarious position hovering between life and death. She had sat his friends down in the waiting room and gently and carefully prepared them for their visit. They had all come bearing gifts—tiny beanie baby animals, a collection trend among his friends at that time. They had to see him, and they had to leave something for him. They desperately wanted him to know that they had been there and they loved him. After they left, I gathered the tiny stuffed monkeys, dogs, and cats. Each friend had tried to find a special one, something unique. Adam rarely was given two of the same. Each day I took one of those soft and cuddly creatures and placed it inside Adam's fist, the position his hands assumed in the midst of his medically induced coma.

Those stuffed animals came home with us, first placed carefully on bookshelves in Adam's new bedroom, our converted dining room on the first floor. The visits from friends continued for months, and the pile of beanie babies grew. A few were stolen by our Chihuahua, Rudy, whose aggressive little mouth fit perfectly around the tiny bodies of these stuffed creatures. Rudy would find one and take off as fast as his short legs could carry him, usually with one of us in hot pursuit. It was impossible to pry them from his mouth, and once he had one entrapped in his mouth, he would tenaciously chew to his heart's content. It was hardly a respectful gesture.

I would show Adam his gifts, but he was terribly locked in his trauma in those early days and months, and he took little pleasure in them. These gifts were more about the giving than the receiving. I gave them a visible presence not for the sake of Adam but for the sake of his friends.

I learned to accept that Adam no longer had a need or desire for trinkets and collectibles. My transformed son lives only in the present moment now, with a few hints of the past and no thought of the future.

HOME SWEET HOME

Our daughter arrived for a visit. Rudy and Chloe, our ever vigilant Chihuahuas, heard her car in the driveway and welcomed her with piercing yaps. I peeked through the window, checking her out from a safe distance. Five fingers, five toes. . . no, I was looking for the face. Was she frowning? Grimacing? Smiling? Placid? I had her in full view now—my beautiful girl—tall, slender, perfectly highlighted blonde hair, wearing tight black yoga pants and tee shirt accented with gold sandals. She slowly approached the house, our new Cape Cod house, glancing here and there. Many new blossoms had appeared since her last visit—blue hydrangeas, daisies, a multitude of daylilies in vibrant deep red, yellow, and orange. She smiled and touched the nearest bush. She seemed pleased until her feet landed in the grass, the ever so slightly too-long patch of grass that graced our front yard. And then the "look"—the tired, cranky lines—crept over her face.

She muttered through the open window, "Dad, why hasn't this lawn been mowed? My friends are visiting tomorrow and I want everything to look nice."

She entered through the front door, continuing her inspection … no greetings yet. Her father and I were sitting in the great room, watching her. The massage table was positioned off to the side, piled high with pillows, wedges, and props, all necessary equipment for Adam's comfort during his many hours of therapy each day. Generally, he was positioned in front of the big-screen TV under the skylights, the light and warmth soothing during his therapy.

Aimee looked at Adam's "stuff" with a weary sigh. "Does this have to be here? Can't you put it away?" Unfortunately, in this moment, I read her subtle message: "Can't you make him better any faster? When will this stuff not be here anymore?" Her impatience with her brother's recovery bubbles over. She can't see all of the subtle and impressive changes. He can't talk to her; he can't walk with her. This is what she sees. She wants her brother back, as black and white as that.

Here we go.

I tried to step back after being instantaneously triggered by her words. She spent the morning sitting for her CPA exam. Aimee has achieved huge milestones in her 25 years. She finished in the top 10% of her high school class; she graduated magna cum laude from Bentley University; she worked full time while she finished her master's degree, and now she was completing her CPA. She worked for a large corporate accounting firm and had been studying every extra moment, if there is any spare time when you work in corporate accounting. She was "stressed to the max," in her words to me every time we spoke on the phone. I attempted on many occasions to coax her to slow down. She was too tired, and I was worried about her. Aimee sets goals for herself and tenaciously pursues them. She is an achiever, this daughter of mine. She is caught up in this whirlwind and almost never stops. Her beloved Tiki, a 25-pound white furball designer mutt, is her only source of constant comfort. He grounds her. He is a love, my "grandpuppy." I remember wondering if she would have the patience, time, and energy for a dog, but she embraced this rambunctious dog, and he loves her with absolute enthusiasm. Unfortunately, his calming spirit was not with her this visit.

With my mother's heart, I watched my firstborn. Each time she visits, we must go through this dance—a recalibration, an adjustment, a decompression. When Aimee leaves our home, our life, she removes herself completely. She forgets. In her other life, she sinks herself in deeply. Then when she approaches the family home, reality slowly creeps into her consciousness and she remembers. Our life is not normal. She must ease into it. I forget this.

The dance steps seemed so clumsy this time. She was exhausted. We tripped and fell over each other. I am always so happy to see her. I wanted to talk; I asked too many questions; she was not ready. I closed my eyes; I waited for the storm to pass. I love my daughter deeply. This discordance is never comfortable. My husband went to the kitchen and returned with a glass of white wine. He said, "Sit, Aimee and I'll get you something to eat." He knows how to soothe her; I get trapped in my offended feelings. If only I could figure out how to meet both of our needs simultaneously.

Many hours later, after two glasses of wine, much chatter and emotional discharge, and a long foot massage from our resident therapist, Maribeth, Aimee finally landed. I was sitting comfortably now, and I continued my vigil. I watched her as she hovered over an art project she had just created for our new house. She looked relaxed; decompressed. I waited for this precious daughter to soften, to peel off those layers of tension. She had molded a stepping stone to place alongside our fish pond, embedding the stone with brilliant colored gems. She had carved the words "HOME SWEET HOME."

A few days later, after Aimee returned to her home outside of Boston, I found a letter I had written to her on her 21st birthday. It was a beautiful reminder for me about the role of our daughter in our life.

My dearest Aimee,

In the minutes and hours after your birth I remember my fear. I said, "Nurse, please take this tiny one back now. I don't think I'm ready to be a mother yet. Are you sure that she's mine?" Yes, they all assured me that I had indeed given birth to this screaming, pink-faced bundle. I took you home, holding my fears close to my heart. You wailed for months, pleading with me to listen to your many needs. . . feed me, change me, hold me, wash me and love me.

You gave me a crash course in mothering; no easy transition for you. You said, "You're my mother. Take care of me." Fortunately for you I ended up loving you.

Aimee, I cherished the thumb-sucking, blanket tugging curly blond-haired little girl who loved to have her feet rubbed. I adored the bouncing, disciplined muscle-toned gymnast who later became a star field hockey and softball player. I loved your five best friends who filled our home with much needed teen-age giggles and energy. And, now, I am in awe of the beautiful, ambitious, independent, fun-loving young woman you have become.

You never allowed me to wallow in my fears. No matter what was happening in our family life you demanded my attention. Had I not engaged in this dance with you I would never have discovered my strength which ultimately helped to prepare me for the biggest challenge in my life—life after Adam's accident.

Aimee, you are my reality check. All you ever wanted through high school and college was a sense of normalcy. You embraced concrete milestones—friends, sports, car, jobs, boyfriends and vacations. I could hear you even when you didn't say this out loud, "Don't forget me! I need your time, energy and love. I won't walk away or hide or act out. . ." Your will to survive and thrive was incredible.

Today, on your birthday, I offer my deepest gratitude to you for initiating me into motherhood and insisting, over the years, that I master the role.

I love you,
Momma

THE WEDDING

My daughter grabbed the window seat and impatiently tossed her bag under the seat in front of her. She turned to me and said, "Now, exactly why are we going to this wedding? You know that I would rather be anywhere but on this plane to Cleveland."

I perfectly understood her sentiment, and, despite her contrary attitude, I was grateful that she was with me. My insides felt like tight rubber bands, and the questions filtering through my mind seemed endless: How can I look at them? How will I celebrate with any generosity of spirit? Can I forgive them? Can they forgive me? Will they visit my son now?

Aimee and I landed in the dark, rented a car in the dark, and eventually, not without mishap, found the designated gathering place—a lovely old inn owned and managed by one of my nephews. The lump in my throat was as hard as a rock, and I coached myself, "Breathe through your nose, Sharon, NOW."

We were the last to arrive. The others—from Alaska, Florida, Pennsylvania, Connecticut, New York, and Ohio—had previously met for dinner at another location. There was no quiet or unobtrusive way to make an entrance. My daughter lagged behind me. Somewhere in this room ahead of us were 21 family members—two brothers and their families, three sisters and their families, and my sister-in-law (deceased brother's wife) and her family. This would be the first wedding of our children.

I had received the notice marking the date of the wedding several months before. It had been followed by a phone call—actually, several phone calls—from my oldest brother—his 37-year-old son was to be married. My brother really wanted me to attend, and he assured me that he could be relentlessly persuasive if necessary. I labored over my decision, sifting through painful thoughts and memories of unmet expectations. I had to continually remind myself how much work I had done to make peace with the absence of extended family in my life. This could be a true test.

Adam was the only missing link. He was not able to travel by plane, and the car drive to Ohio was just too long. I carefully planned my response to all who asked about him. I carried his picture—one with his huge smile, laughing eyes, and healthy, glowing skin. And, yes, I would casually mention that he was still recovering from his brain injury.

When we entered the room, we were greeted warmly. We exchanged polite kisses and hugs. A few tears spilled over, even though I had promised my daughter that I would not cry. Aimee eventually made her way over to her cousins. I watched her move away from me. She is beautiful and carries herself with elegant poise. People seemed awestruck by her presence. Then I remembered how clearly we see the passage of time through our children. As I moved from brother to brother, sister to sister, and then to my nieces and nephews, I asked, "Would you like to see my son?" Each time, it seems, his picture was held with reverence, and the comments flowed: "He looks so good" and "Is he always this happy?" And a few say, "Tell me about Adam."

The day of the wedding was filled with moments of connection. The wedding began with a very moving tribute to the bride's father, who had died three years before. I took these minutes to shed my repressed tears, and no one noticed.

During the ceremony, after the bride and groom exchanged vows, the pastor turned to the families of the couple and asked us all to stand and announce "en masse" a resounding "We do" to support and affirm the union of this couple. I thought, *This is what it feels like to stand together as a family.*

And then the snapshots… my sisters and I gathered, heads together, arms around each other. Two sisters are breast cancer survivors, and, well, I am a survivor of another kind. My two brothers joined us, and we were six. We had been seven until 18 years before, when the second-oldest brother had died. Our youngest brother was 16 when our mother died, and our oldest brother had been 16 when our father died. As a family, we have endured much loss, but that day, as we stood together, we were touching and we were all smiling. I thought, *Is this what it feels like to stand together as family?*

A lighter moment and a beautiful snapshot… Aimee and two of her cousins gathered in play. They dabbed frosting from the wedding cake on each of their noses, laughed, took pictures, and danced together. They also spent time examining each other's features—finding similarities in their eyes and the shapes of their faces.

There was time that I am grateful was not captured by a camera. I was feeling tired, overwhelmed, overstimulated, and polite-talked-out. I left the reception to seek some kind of solitude and refuge. The weekend was almost over. I had almost pulled it off … no one could see the conflict inside me. I returned and sat near one of my nephews, who was sitting off to the side, away from the loud music and dancing. He was 15 and so shy he could barely maintain eye contact. He looked at me , moved close, and wrapped his arm around me. We sat in quiet for awhile. And again, I thought, *Is this what it feels like to stand with family?*

In hindsight, the anticipation leading up to this momentous event threatened to suffocate me, but the moments of connection kept me breathing. I have two brothers and three sisters, and we are bonded, for better or worse, until death do us part.

KAUAI

Aloha, my spirit breath greets you—an invocation of the Divine. I entered the island of Kauai at Lihue, very close to where Hawaiian folklore identifies the entry of new spirits. Aloha!

I dashed off the plane, wired with adrenaline from my excitement and plagued with achiness from 14 hours of sitting. I did not look around, did not stop at baggage claim because I had stuffed everything into my carryon suitcase. I had a mission—get to my rental car and find my friends' home. I jumped into the car and called their home; no one answered. Where were they? I left a message and headed away from the airport, peeking at the Mapquest directions, absolutely distracted by the stunning, exquisite landscape—the lush green mountains, the blue-green ocean waters—in front of me, to the sides of me. And then I was lost.

My phone rang. "Where are you?" Terri was at the airport, and three flights had landed. No Sharon. "Pull over, I will find you."

Someone who knows both of us very well later commented, "Sharon would never expect someone to meet her," and "Terri would never expect not to meet someone who was visiting."

We laughed, we hugged, we cried. While Terri had waited for me, she had picked up her partner, Jenny, so we all gathered in greeting. A lei of white orchids was slipped over my head and a basket of longon—a succulent, refreshing grape-like fruit—was presented. I could not stop smiling and laughing. And this was just the beginning.

We arrived at their home. It was lovely and comfortable, like them, and I felt at home immediately. These two friends are incredibly gracious, with open hearts. They could not do enough for me—cooking, decorating my guest room with flowers. Terri had designated herself as recreation director.

My first day began with an ayurvedic warm oil treatment focused on my "third eye." I loved it, closing my eyes, allowing my brow to be bathed in oil. The therapist was a quiet presence. I could feel her as she poured the warm oil, but I barely heard her movement as she moved about. A craniosacral session with a very skilled practitioner followed on the second day. She embraced me when we first met, and I remember thinking, *Is this an island thing or has my friend nurtured this affection in them before I even appeared?* This therapist immediately diagnosed a very serious energetic misalignment. I had flown 6,000 miles in a crowded, compressed airplane. No, this was just the superficial layer—the truth went deeper, of course, to 10 years of serious and constant caretaking.

Another day, I was offered a lomi lomi massage. The history behind this Hawaiian massage is magical. People were massaged until they felt that they had discharged enough, cleared enough to move on, to be transformed. The therapist began with a beautiful Hawaiian chant, and I felt moved into a sacred space. I knew then that I would be open to her touch and to receive whatever she offered and release whatever I could. At the end, she quietly asked, "How are you, Sharon?" and I answered, "I am fine, just fine."

Each morning I would sit in my friends' front room, sipping my Kauai coffee, looking out at the majestic mountains. One morning it had rained, and I witnessed not just one rainbow, but two, almost side by side. Each day seemed to bring something new and beautiful. We drove from one end of the island to the other, from one side to the other side. Terri and Jenny took me to their favorite beaches, all with magical stories. We visited the Waimea Canyon—a landscape that literally takes your breath away. One of my favorite moments took place with Jenny at the Kilauea lighthouse, where I saw both a humpback whale and an albatross. I found myself at that moment, without restraint, shrieking with joy. Who had I become on this tiny Hawaiian island?

I had not expected any of the bodywork or even the tour around the island. I had anxiously left Adam and Phil in our new home on Cape Cod for ten days to spend time with two women I love in the warmth of the sun, the surf of the ocean, the splendor of the mountains—an exquisite background. We had intimate breakfasts during which we would share our dreams from the luxurious cool nights of sleep. One afternoon, Terri and I wrote with a small group of women sitting on a lanai open to a refreshing tropical breeze. I spent one morning hiking a mountain with Terri—and a hike is never just a hike with Terri. She was waiting, and after many days of bodywork, sun, reading, and traveling around the island, I was ready. I stood in the middle of the trail, and she coaxed it out. "You need to say it, Sharon."

I took a deep breath and forced the words out. "I acknowledge that my life is hard. My life is very hard. As I work with Adam, I cannot be attached to an outcome. I must stay in the present. My mantra is 'Move forward, slow and steady.' The changes we notice in Adam are barely perceptible to others. They continue to see a young man who cannot speak, who cannot use his arms and legs. It's lonely, but we know that we have chosen the best path for his healing. Adam's caretaking is physically demanding, and we have to acknowledge our aging bodies. Yes, it's difficult." Terri stood in the middle of the trail and held me.

I left these women and this island of Kauai, replenished in body, mind, and spirit. I felt grateful, and I returned to my son and my husband eager to reenter the rhythm and routine of our life. I choose this life every day. Mahalo—may you be in Divine Breath.

ADAM'S ODE

I am bored.
I announce this is in many obnoxious ways.
I hear footsteps nearing my room.
I draw my eyes away from the television and fixate on the fan
above my bed or on the empty wall beside my bed. These
objects hold no real interest to me, of course; that is the point.
I am protesting.
I can feel a devilish expression of delight creeping over my face.
Who will play my game?
Who will draw me away from the fan or the wall?
Who will call my name, search into my eyes, and laugh at my
creative call for attention?
Who will be my friend?
Who will tease me for my newfound prowess?
Who will join me in this private joke?

I am alone.
I am lonely.
I am bored.
I would like a friend—not a mother, not a father, not a sister,
not a therapist or a dog or a cat.
Someone my age, a guy friend—young man to young man.
He could come to my house, come to my room, connect with

my eyes—this is how I speak.

Take me for a ride.

Take me for a walk along the shining sea bike path.

I love it there—the warm sun, the smell of the ocean air, the screeching of the gulls. I love it all; I want it all.

I sit in my chair, close my eyes, and breathe. I feel part of something magnificent.

I become one with the sea.

I am full of ideas.

I can see myself at a local baseball game. I remember standing at first base, squatting in position, my long legs spread as far apart as possible. Every tag up was within my reach. Not to brag, but I could extend and jump and catch just about anything.

My mother watches the Red Sox with me, and she is well-intentioned, but it's not the same as watching it with a buddy, young man to young man.

I like going to the movies, too—the large screen, high-definition stereo surround sound, the buttery smell of popcorn and the buzz of the crowded theater.

A guy movie.

A sports movie.

I need a friend.

I know it must be hard. I sit in a wheelchair and I need to be transported in a clumsy, gas-guzzling van. I need help with everything, really.

But let me tell you a few things about myself. I am, without a doubt, one of the most incredible listeners you will ever meet.

I can see you.

I can understand you.

I can feel you—my senses are sharply tuned.

I am not afraid to look at you, to really look into your eyes.

I will speak to you if you become my friend—my eyes to your eyes.

I am easily amused, a captive audience.
I love slapstick comedy.
I love to laugh.
I invite you to be my friend.

AN ITCH THAT HE
CANNOT SCRATCH

The eye doctor examined Adam and nodded approvingly while he completed the yearly check-up. "Just one thing," he said, "besides a small change in his prescription." He pointed to Adam's eyelids, upper and lower, focusing on a small amount of redness and gritty material. He named the condition and said, with a good degree of compassion, "I just want you to know that this may be itchy for him." I swallowed hard.

Is this true? Does Adam have an itch that he cannot scratch? He has very defined contractures in his arms—bent at the elbow, bent at the wrist, and locked tight against his chest. During the weeks and months after the accident, he pulled his arms and wrists inward, an emphatic gesture of self-protection. No amount of botox, casting, splinting, or range of motion has made any enduring impact. He cannot touch his nose, bring a fork or spoon to his mouth, brush his teeth, scratch his ear, or rub his eye.

Adam is dependent on me for all of his physical needs. We visit the dentist every three months to remove plaque from his teeth. I receive the compliments for his beautiful teeth, brushed and flossed to perfection. I wash his face each morning and night with botanicals, and he has beautiful skin. My daughter notices and compliments me. I take him to the hairdresser, and

I decide what to do with his thick, wavy hair. Buzz the sides and back and layer the top. He watches in the mirror as the hair falls on his shoulders. Before the accident, he was very particular about his hair. He mashed the front bangs flat on his forehead; I thought that it looked silly, but I kept quiet. I prepare his foods and feed him—protein, vegetables, fruits, and carbohydrates—a balanced diet. As a child, he lived on bowls of cereal and slices of toast with peanut butter. Now, I choose his food and bring the spoon to his lips. He has been known to spit it out if he doesn't like the taste. I am in charge, and sometimes he just doesn't like it.

It pains me to know that my son may have been experiencing itchy eyes. I, however, cannot know this to be absolutely true. When I hold onto this thought, I beat myself up. I feel negligent and sad. I see my son as powerless, helpless, and tortured. I need to let this go. I appreciate the doctor for recognizing the possibility and telling me in a gentle way. This morning, I warmed up a washcloth, poured baby shampoo on the corner, and carefully lathered my son's eyes, moving over them slowly. No more itch; problem solved for today.

RUDY

I was inconsolable. My grief felt open-ended. I had lost my beloved Rudy. He had been with us for 10 years. I felt his absence and the absence of every other being that had graced my life. I missed my father, my mother, my brother. I held Rudy as he died, and I remembered those other moments of death that I was so privileged to bear witness to. I had known that my dog was seriously ill, just as I had known that my mother and brother were ill, but each passing is jolting in an unexpected way... just one more year, one more week, one more day. I was not ready to let him go. And then the realization and acceptance entered my heart that indeed he was ready and needing to move beyond this life. He left, and I still lingered with the "if only" and the "should" and the "ought," the pattern reminiscent of my other life losses.

I believed that if I could recount his life, perhaps I could get beyond his death. He was four months old when Aimee and I met him. One of my sisters had convinced us that a Chihuahua would be the perfect match for our family. We only meant to have one, though he ended up with a playmate less than six months later. We chose him because he made us laugh. He was called an "apple-head"—tan and white with floppy ears, which were very un-Chihuahua-like, short legs, and a svelte little body. He walked with a proud, brazen strut. The timing was perfect. It was the second year after Adam's accident, and we were bringing life and laughter into our home. Rudy was a squirming ball of energy, running all over the house, playing "fetch" with a little Chihuahua stuffed animal whose eyes had been gnawed away by Rudy's little teeth. I have memories of him curled into a tiny ball after he had exhausted himself. When Adam lay on the floor during therapy, Rudy would insert himself between Adam's legs and sleep undisturbed.

And such a strong personality—this dear dog, Rudy, lived for food and sleep, and his wish, whether I ever really admitted it to myself, was my command. He woke up at 5:00 a.m., hurried to the door to relieve himself, and ran to the kitchen to await his breakfast. Twice a day, by the clock—exact time each day, he demanded a meal. And the rituals—he licked the bowl clean at least five times. Then he attacked the surrounding floor, devouring any tiny leftover morsel of food. Finally, surreptitiously, of course, he slowly moved over to the dish belonging to Chloe, our other Chihuahua. If he was lucky, she had left him a bit, some gravy maybe. Ah, the joy of those daily rituals.

When Rudy was new to our life, Aimee was quite taken with him and his then "charming" characteristics. Rudy, of course, adored Aimee. Aimee would beg me to bring him to her field hockey games. I would zip him into my jacket, and his head would pop out just enough to greet his fans. We tried to make this a habit, but he just never got comfortable socializing with strangers. Rudy was clear that he preferred a small, close-knit group, our family, to be precise.

I initially saw him as Adam's dog, some little being to keep Adam company in between therapies and during the long, sometimes sleepless, nights. Not to be. Rudy had other ideas. He chose me. He chose to love me almost exclusively. It was hard sometimes. Other people really wanted to hold him, kiss him, and sit with him. It was not to be; he became nippy, growly, and disgruntled. A one-woman dog he was.

His unrelenting devotion was remarkable. Sometimes I was impatient with his demands, and many times he had to hear, "Not now, Rudy. It's not time for food or bed." He reluctantly complied, but not before he stood on his hind legs and swatted his nose with his front paws in complete frustration.

There was just one more thing—I did appreciate his protectiveness toward Chloe, his adopted playmate of nine years. I would tell him to find her, and out the door he would run, seeking that "undependable" sister of his. When we needed to kennel the dogs during our travels with Adam, Rudy was the "brave lion" who protected Chloe from any intruders into their space within the confines of their crate. I know that Rudy didn't quite know what to do around Adam, but he was never mean, dutifully laying kisses on Adam's cheeks and hands when requested. I also loved how he ran out to meet Adam's van when Adam returned from trips.

We found the perfect place for Rudy's resting spot, right below Adam's window in the gardens in front of our beautiful Cape Cod home. I am so grateful for Rudy's 10 years of unconditionally loving companionship. He was the consummate loyal supporter.

MY HERO

Each night, I tend to Adam, washing his face, brushing his teeth, giving him his homeopathic remedies. I carefully place the foam and bladders on his chest, stomach, and pelvis and hook him up to the ABR machines. They purr alongside him all night long, the air bladders gently inflating and deflating against his body. I darken his room, put something very boring on TV, and slip away for an hour. At exactly 9:00 most nights, I creep back in, usually finding Adam close to sleep and dreams. I kiss his forehead and whisper, "Goodnight, my young man. You are my hero."

He has been my hero for a very long time, and I clearly remember the incredibly dramatic event years before his accident that elevated him to this level in my eyes. The trophy lies deep in a box in a corner in the basement. I haven't looked at it for many years, but I know that it is there.

Adam's hockey team was playing in a tournament about an hour's drive from home. He was on an exclusive travel team, and we spent many weekends driving all over the state. His team was good, and Adam was an excellent goalie. On the way to games, he was usually anxious. His father would drive, and I would be relegated to the backseat. When Adam was in this precarious state of mind, Phil was his best companion. He read Adam like a book; he knew when to talk, when to leave him alone, when to indulge his every wish. I paled in comparison, mostly because Adam's behavior drove me crazy. I didn't want to enable his moodiness, I would tell myself. And then Adam would tell me how to behave at the ice rink. He swore that he could hear me when I cheered, yelled, coached him from the sidelines. I would sit in the bleachers in a huge ice rink with lots of noise and many, many cheering fans and I was expected to be silent.

On this particular weekend, Adam played probably three games. I don't remember many details, only the final minutes. To win the tournament Adam's team needed to win one more game. The game was exciting, and both teams were playing extremely well. I often held my breath; rarely could I take my eyes off my son. I tried not to holler and scream, but I could hear the words springing from my mouth, "Adam, pay attention. They're coming. Stop them!" And he would watch, move forward, and stop each puck with his stick, glove, or skate. Some came so close that they needed just one tiny opening. I never worried about him getting hurt. He was covered from head to toe with protection, and his defense players protected him too. He had excellent hand-eye coordination, and he could cover the net with his body and stick.

No score. The last period ended, and someone had to win the game and, ultimately, the tournament. A shoot-out was the necessary play. Each team would have five chances to score, using its best forward and its best goalie. Adam was the goalie. I wanted to watch, but I couldn't. I peeked with one eye. He stopped one, two, three, and four. By then, the whole rink was packed with spectators and everyone was screaming. My eyes were uncovered, and so was my mouth. I screamed with everyone. Adam's teammate had just scored one goal, and if Adam stopped the next and last shot, his team would win. Everybody suddenly quieted down as the forward from the opposing team approached Adam. Adam was ready. The puck was in the air, heading to the goal, and Adam's right hand jolted up at the precise time. People gasped, and Adam casually dropped the puck out of his glove onto the ice. His teammates rushed him and piled on top. They had won. The crowd went wild. I went wild.

We all waited for the boys in the outer room. They walked in as a team, and everyone cheered. Adam saw me; I smiled, and he mouthed, "I heard you, Mom." We had a quiet ride home. Adam was exhausted and very pleased with himself. When we arrived home, he fell asleep immediately. I bent down and kissed my sleeping boy's forehead and whispered, "Goodnight, my son. You are my hero."

ADAM'S ONE AND ONLY

She tracked us down through our daughter, through Facebook. Megan was now 23, a registered nurse, and married, with a 10-month-old son. She was Adam's first and only girlfriend.

They were 12 years old in 1998 and in the sixth grade. Adam definitely wanted a girlfriend; he had awakened to the charms of the opposite sex. Despite being extremely busy with sports, school, and his guy friends, he had the will and the wish. The dances at the local YMCA nurtured this young coupling. One weekend, Adam talked my husband into taking him on a shopping spree for some "cool clothes." Phil was hardly the fashionista, but Adam had him firmly wrapped around his little finger. He would get whatever he wanted. They returned with baggy jeans, name-brand oversized shirts, and the latest Nike sneakers. Adam's lanky, athletic body did not exactly compliment this style.

The romance started with frantically sketched notes, all folded up in tightly constructed squares. A few times, I must admit, I found a note or two in Adam's jeans, removed them before they turned into mush in the washer, and, without hesitation or remorse, carefully attempted to unfold them. Much to my chagrin, I rarely managed to unlock the code, and the note would ripe into pieces. The notes were followed by long phone calls. Adam was not a chatterbox, so I often wondered what filled those minutes. One time, I stood outside his bedroom door, always tightly closed when he was on the phone with Megan, and pressed my ear against the wood. I heard music playing, and then I put it all together. Adam was playing love songs to Megan; he didn't have to talk to her.

At that time I thought that I was a good parent, somewhat on the strict side when I announced to both of my children, "No dating in middle school; only group gatherings." With this group model in place, I set off one weekend with a car full of kids. Adam invited Megan, her sister, and Barrett—two boys and two girls. It was near Halloween, and Adam had asked me to drive them to a local amusement park for a haunted evening. Adam was clear that he wanted me to be the driver; his father was not very proficient at social niceties. I tended to keep conversations going, and Adam preferred this to the awkward silence that might occur if the kids were left to their own devices. My instructions were clear: I was to keep the atmosphere comfortable in the car, and when we arrived at the park, I was to disappear while they explored. We were to meet later at a designated spot. It was dusk soon after we drove into the park, and I remember thinking, *God, what do middle school kids do in the dark, and should I discreetly follow them?* I did watch them climb onto a haunted hayride, and then I lost sight of them for several hours, not that I wasn't looking. I must have walked for miles that night, surrounded by Frankensteins, ghouls, vampires, and zombies. I waited at the meeting place long before the appointed time; they arrived excited and breathless. On the way home, the car was dark and very quiet, and I was left imagining these two very young and exhausted couples clandestinely holding hands.

I don't recall the duration of this romance, perhaps a few months. Adam broke up with Megan because his friends didn't like her and he could not tolerate the teasing. Middle school is brutal. Adam cried for days, and I remember feeling curious about this. At the young age of 12, why such grief?

Megan called several months after Adam's accident. I assumed that she must hate him; he had broken her heart. Perhaps catastrophic events allow one to drop all of that.

She visited a few times with her twin sister. Megan would chat with me, and her twin would just sit and smile. They were beautiful girls. They always greeted Adam warmly and quickly moved away from his wheelchair. What 12-year-old knows how to act in this type of situation? What adult knows?

I don't know when the visits stopped, but Megan called me from time to time, just checking in. She visited by herself before she left for college, this time driving her car up the driveway. At school, away from home and the safety of community, she wrote me letters. I responded a few times and sent her a picture or two of Adam. She seemed to have a need to know, to share some piece of Adam's reality even if I had to be the conduit. Now she is married and continues to need to know.

CERAMIC TO CLAY

"Ceramic to clay," Leonid said as he stood over Adam's prone body. "Well, no, that's not quite right. It's more like hard-glazed ceramic to clay." He was describing Adam's physical changes as he moves through this ABR process designed to restore and normalize his severely distorted structure. Leonid loves to create metaphors to help parents better visualize this remarkable rehabilitative therapy. I am the type of person who requires a metaphor to get the point. Leonid and I understood each other. Over the years, Adam's rigid, spastic, contracted body was softening, moving from hard ceramic to soft clay. The ABR mantra (I am very fond of mantras) is "volume, mobility, function": You must have increased volume to have mobility, and you must have mobility to have function—basic biomechanical principles. I have a simple understanding of a very complex process.

We have packed our van 20 times now, traveling to Montreal for evaluation and training. My anticipation and excitement never diminishes. Why would it? Adam's progress has been consistent and significant. We are not alone. Across the world, hundreds of families practice this therapy, and word is spreading.

This evaluation was particularly validating and motivating. "This is better, better and better," Leonid said. He gently manipulated Adam's head, neck, arms, and legs, searching for new volume and mobility. Adam's shoulder girdle, spine, rib cage, and pelvis are checked and rechecked. New volume, elongation, and movement into proper musculoskeletal alignment are documented through video and photos. Leonid smiled and said, "The pace of Adam's response is picking up." I heard, "We are no longer at the beginning of this process. The hard-glazed ceramic is softening into clay."

Leonid is excited by Adam, his progress and his unusually good health, and this, in turn, excites us. It is not untrue or unfair to say that it is highly doubtful that Adam would be alive today were it not for the path we have chosen for his recovery. For one long moment, I think about all of the treatments, therapists, and aides who have contributed to Adam's general well-being. We have continued to be mindful of the body-mind-spirit connection in everything we offer to Adam and ourselves. We complement ABR with acupuncture, homeopathy, cell-salts, and shiatsu. After 11 years, we still consider Adam to be in an active state of rehabilitation.

Leonid completed the exam, complimented Phil and me on our brave move to use two ABR machines in addition to the manual exercises, and sent us on to the training. I didn't leave without asking one final question. Before this trip, Leonid had alerted parents to some upcoming changes. He is one man, one incredibly committed and passionate man, and he is spreading himself too thin. With a lump in my throat I asked, "When will we see you again?"

He said, "One year." The panic didn't arrive yet. I was afraid that the answer would be "never again." The reality of his "one year" response set in after we returned home. I calculated what exactly that would mean. We would not see Leonid until we had finished approximately 900 manual hours and 8,000 machine hours.

I was spinning for a while when we returned home, energized by the progress and depleted by the travel and hard work from the training. Full-blown panic hit soon enough. I reached out to my dear friend and mentor as I spiraled down into that unfortunately familiar place of fear that is triggered so easily by change and perceived loss.

Dear Terri,

We are such complicated human beings, aren't we? The minute I think that I finally have it all figured out—knowing how to balance my life, knowing how to keep moving forward with Adam, feeling stability, then POW!

Leonid is pulling back, out of necessity, of course, to work more effectively and efficiently in the delivery of ABR. I am screaming in my head, "No! We need you! We need your physical presence, your comforting metaphors. No one can deliver like you can!" I am in serious panic and the questions keep flowing. Can we keep this going? One more year? Two more years? Many more years? Sustainability. . . feeling so insecure.

I look at Adam. I mean REALLY LOOK AT HIM. I see cognitive brightness, clarity, joy, boisterous vocalizing AND he still looks locked in this body, though it has softened and released on so many levels. We have the tools to help this process. Do we have the fortitude and longevity necessary to assist him?

Don't know what I need. I do feel afraid and very fragile. I have been here too many times. . .

Terri responded within hours:

Complicated and complex. . .
Well, I am not surprised to hear of the crash.
The truth is: you have been on an adrenaline
rush for 10 years now!!!!!!

. . . this time
with all the skills and tools you have
you are being called
NOT to re-create the buzz
but to RE-ALIGN
with your spirit
which is the process you have been in
and now are called
to integrate that sustainably

go direct
to spirit
every day
every moment
in fact, this whole thing with Adam, his karmic
manifestation
is because he said that he needed to align with
his spirit. . .and finish off
the karmic debt of previous
actions he took.

You see
It is PERFECT that Leonid is stretching out
the assessments
because

YOU CANNOT GO TO HUMANS for what only resides in SOURCE
each of us has to make this relationship our-selves
authentically

a radical re-alignment is taking place
you go direct to SOURCE
(WALKING BY THE OCEAN, WRITING, QUIET TIME, NOT
RUSHING, DEEP INNER LISTENING)

. . .time does not matter to spirit
a year a day
spirits reside infinitely
this is what you see when Adam smiles
a being aligned with his spirit

yes, it is hard. . . that is what tears are for. . .to touch the rough times
in this humanness and wash it away. . .
And to reach again and again into this subtle spaciousness of spirit
aligned with self.

I printed out her e-mail and walked to the ocean. I read and reread her words, and I could not stop crying. What was I hearing? Why was I crying? The words about Adam and his karmic manifestation always bring me comfort. My husband and I were offered this explanation for Adam's life challenge many years ago, and then and now, it consoles us; it resonates as true. He chose this human situation and he also chose us as his parents. He had faith in our ability to handle this journey. We are learning how to move away from distraction, painful thoughts, and expectations. We are learning how to live a life without fear, no matter what circumstances present themselves, because we know that we are anchored in something much bigger than ourselves and our singular lives. These are not easy lessons; they take time and patience.

Taking care of Adam is good and honest work. It is our passion; it is our path. Our son is a formidable teacher. He has mastered the art of "being in the moment, loving what is." A memory eased its way into my heart. My son was about nine years old. He and I had decided to take a ski lesson together with a small group of people. He listened and practiced a bit and then split from the group, flying down the mountain. I saw him with his hand on his hip, looking up at me who was still safely embedded in the group, waiting for the courage to break out.

I walked toward Falmouth Harbor. Not by coincidence but by fortune, I had a startling experience with a red-tailed hawk. Almost 11 years ago, an adolescent red-tailed hawk provided Terri with a sign to enter our life. On this day, this bird of prey, which in Native American animal medicine represents truth, clarity, and strength, appeared right on cue. I saw the mature hawk flying toward the water. I turned and watched as the hawk, wings fully open, hung suspended in the air for a long, long moment, holding steady against the powerful ocean wind. A passing motorist stopped and watched with me. "Magnificent," he said.

"Yes," I said with a nod. "Magnificent."

LaVergne, TN USA
17 November 2010
205336LV00001B/3/P

9 781608 447589